"As I read Lisa Appelo's book *Life* (
grateful for this powerful resource. Th
hope, and experience. If you or some
season, this book is practical, spiritua

Suzanne Eller, a..., ..., speaker,
and cohost of *More Than Small Talk* podcast

"Scriptures warn us that we will go through trials in this life. Many times, they will knock the wind out of us and threaten to pull us under. Those are the times we most want a lifeline, a hand to hold, a friend who has been there. *Life Can Be Good Again* is exactly that, and Lisa Appelo is that friend. Lisa shares her truth about suffering, along with the hope we have knowing God is with us through it. God walked her through some very dark, difficult places, and she shares with confidence that He will do that for you too."

Dr. Michelle Bengtson, clinical neuropsychologist, podcast host, and author of the award-winning *Breaking Anxiety's Grip: How to Reclaim the Peace God Promises* and *Hope Prevails: Insights from a Doctor's Personal Journey through Depression*

"Lisa Appelo understands suffering. In *Life Can Be Good Again*, she poignantly shares her own pain, offering remarkable insight and practical wisdom on navigating the unthinkable. If you're struggling with the gap between the life you hoped for and the life you're living now, read this inspiring book!"

Vaneetha Rendall Risner, author of *Walking Through Fire: A Memoir of Loss and Redemption*

"*Life Can Be Good Again* is easily one of the best books I've ever read on suffering! An incredibly raw story that is filled with the hope of God's Word, it will encourage even the weariest soul. It doesn't shy away from answering some of the toughest questions we face in hard seasons, and it offers guidance that can only come from someone who has already walked the path. What an encouraging and hope-filled read that helps us to find good again."

Brittany Price Brooker

"Lisa Appelo is the voice of quiet strength and practical hope we need when grief sideswipes us, and our hearts, faith, and hope are in tatters. Lisa's words will encourage and guide you one small, gentle step at a time."

Niki Hardy, national speaker, coach, and author of *Breathe Again: How to Live Well When Life Falls Apart*

"If you've experienced a deep loss or disappointment of any kind, *Life Can Be Good Again* is for you. Lisa Appelo is the wise and trustworthy friend we all need to help us navigate life on the other side of devastating circumstances. This isn't a book of trite platitudes or a prescription for flimsy positivity. Rather, from the battlefield of her own unimaginable pain, Lisa gently guides us with biblical truth toward an unshakable hope that life really can be good again."

Becky Keife, author of *The Simple Difference* and *No Better Mom for the Job*

"Not everyone is qualified to offer encouragement to others when life falls apart. Some offer insufficient and sometimes incentive words that never penetrate the pain of the moment. That is not the case with Lisa. She knows and understands what it is like when your life is completely and unexpectedly altered forever. She has weathered the unthinkable and charted a practical and real path for others to follow. Her book is a tangible reminder for anyone who is dreading the present and pessimistic about the future that life can (and will) be good again."

Kia Stephens, author, speaker, and creator of Entrusted Women

"In so many ways, I felt like Lisa was writing my story. Her personal experiences and descriptions of trials and grief are on point. Her words serve as an arrow pointing us back to the truth that God is the greatest comforter, and He intends for us to flourish after loss."

Dorina Lazo Gilmore-Young, author, speaker, podcaster

"As a counselor who treats widows and family members who've experienced traumatic grief, I am so excited to now have *Life Can Be Good Again* as a recommended resource. Lisa Appelo's story and approach provides much-needed hope for those suffering when life hits hard."

Michelle Nietert, LPC-S, author of *Loved and Cherished* and *Make Up Your Mind*, host of *Raising Mentally Healthy Kids* podcast

LIFE CAN BE GOOD AGAIN

PUTTING YOUR WORLD
BACK TOGETHER
AFTER IT ALL FALLS APART

LISA APPELO

BETHANYHOUSE
a division of Baker Publishing Group
Minneapolis, Minnesota

Published by Bethany House Publishers
11400 Hampshire Avenue South
Minneapolis, Minnesota 55438
www.bethanyhouse.com

Bethany House Publishers is a division of
Baker Publishing Group, Grand Rapids, Michigan

Printed in the United States of America

Library of Congress Cataloging-in-Publication Data
Names: Appelo, Lisa, author.
Title: Life can be good again : putting your world back together after it all falls apart / Lisa Appelo.
Description: Minneapolis, Minnesota : Bethany House Publishers, a division of Baker Publishing Group, [2022] | Includes bibliographical references.
Identifiers: LCCN 2021053574 | ISBN 9780764239281 (pbk.) | ISBN 9780764240621 (casebound) | ISBN 9781493435760 (ebook)
Subjects: LCSH: Consolation. | Change (Psychology)—Religious aspects—Christianity.
Classification: LCC BV4905.3 .A65 2022 | DDC 248.8/6—dc23/eng/20220106
LC record available at https://lccn.loc.gov/2021053574

Cover design by Susan Zucker

Baker Publishing Group publications use paper produced from sustainable forestry practices and post-consumer waste whenever possible.

22 23 24 25 26 27 28 7 6 5 4 3 2 1

To Ben, Rachel, Nicholas, Seth,
Zachary, Matthew, and Annalise.
The life I wanted for you has been surrendered
to the life God has chosen for you.
Your courage inspires me every day,
and I know your dad would be so proud.
I love you fierce.

Contents

Introduction

The cords of death entangled me;
  the torrents of destruction overwhelmed me.
The cords of the grave coiled around me;
  the snares of death confronted me.
In my distress I called to the LORD;
  I cried to my God for help.
From his temple he heard my voice;
  my cry came before him, into his ears.

Psalm 18:4–6

Hon, it's just a nightmare," I said groggily, still half-asleep.

In the dark hours of early morning, I'd woken to my husband's deep breathing. With my eyes too heavy to open, I extended an arm over to Dan's side of the bed to nudge him from the nightmare. As a mom to seven, I'm a super-light sleeper. It wasn't unusual for me to wake up and stir Dan to turn over so he would stop snoring.

I settled back onto my pillow to drift back to sleep like hundreds of other nights. Instead, I realized this was not his normal snoring but a whole different nightmare of irregular breathing.

I was instantly out of bed and had flipped on the overhead light. I could now see Dan, lying on his back, eyes open and intermittently drawing in long, deep breaths.

I don't have a speck of medical training, but I knew something was very wrong. Had he choked? Was he conscious? Could he see me? My mind raced.

I held my hands to the sides of his face and blurted out questions. "Dan! Can you hear me?"

Dan didn't respond. He didn't move and there was no sign he'd registered any of my questions.

Still sleeping next to him was our four-year-old, Annalise, who crawled into our bed each night, much as I tried to keep her in her own.

Our eldest, nineteen-year-old Ben, had just left to spend the summer in North Carolina as a camp counselor. But my five other children, alarmed at my shouts, came into our room. As circumstances would have it, they had spent the night in the family room right outside our bedroom. The upstairs air conditioner had gone out the day before, making it pretty miserable in Florida's mid-June heat. Since we were leaving for a big family trip the next day—a trip to Maine with extended family to celebrate my parents' fiftieth anniversary—we'd decided to fix the air conditioner when we got back.

I went into crisis management mode. "Nick, call 9-1-1. Rachel, take Annalise and Matt upstairs. Seth, run down and get Mr. Gillespie."

Mr. Gillespie was a neighbor and fireman.

Everyone sprang into action.

Nick put the 9-1-1 operator on speaker phone. Did I know CPR, she asked. I flashed back to early middle school when I practiced chest compressions and mouth-to-mouth on a dummy with my Girl Scout troop, and I had vague memories of practicing again for a baby-sitting course, but all of that had been years ago.

"You'll have to walk me through this," I told the operator.

Our first step was to move Dan off the bed and get him onto the carpet. Dan was a strapping six feet, three inches, and every inch of him solid. Already this task seemed too hard. I lifted Dan's shoulders while sixteen-year-old Nick lifted Dan's middle and we got him to the floor. Later, I learned that twelve-year-old Zach had stepped in to help. On the way to the floor, Dan's head hit the nightstand, and I breathed out prayers and apologies. I wanted to stop and cradle his head, but I had to steel myself to start CPR.

The operator told me where to place my hands on his chest. She began to count out loud as I began compressions. "One, two, three, four, five, six—"

It felt as if part of me was looking down from above, watching the unimaginable take place. *Please tell me I am not giving CPR to my husband, my high school sweetheart, my best friend, and our rock.*

"—seven, eight, nine, ten, eleven—"

"I love you, Dan," I cried out loud as the operator and my son kept counting. If he could still hear me, if this was the last thing he ever heard, I wanted him to know we loved him. "We love you."

"—twelve, thirteen, fourteen, fifteen—" I pushed my palms against his chest with all my weight. *Is this even hard enough? Are my hands in the right place?*

After thirty quick compressions, I pinched Dan's nose between my fingers, laid my mouth over his, and gave him my breath. Deep inhale—mouth over his—long breath out. Deep inhale—mouth over his—long breath out.

"Now you need to check his pulse," the operator instructed.

I checked his wrist first. Nothing. I checked his neck. Nothing. *Surely, it's just that I'm not trained. I just don't know how to find it.*

But the full impact of what was happening was dawning on me. Dan had been perfectly fine days before when the two of us had tacked a little getaway onto one of his business trips. We'd laughed and reminisced while he made phone calls and worked in the car. We'd taken the coastal highway to stop at a favorite restaurant that hadn't changed since our high school dates there. Back home the night before, we had pizza and a routine evening with the kids. Dan hadn't been sick, didn't seem tired, and never appeared winded or in pain.

I had turned in early since I had a big day ahead to get us all ready for the family trip. "I'm going to finish this paperwork for my mom," Dan had said. I told him good-night and tucked into bed like a thousand other nights.

Something had gone terribly wrong in the wee hours of the night.

Before I was even finished with the second round of CPR, the paramedics arrived at our home. *He's in good hands now*, I thought. *Whew, he's going to be so miffed when he wakes up and realizes he has to miss work today.*

I was guided out of the room as paramedics cut open Dan's T-shirt. Pacing in the living room, I prayed out loud: "Lord, have mercy on us. Oh, dear God, have mercy on us." My spirits lifted when I overheard one paramedic say he was getting some good color, and I could hear them placing paddles on his chest, counting, and then the beeps and discharge of the defibrillator.

Before long, they had Dan on a stretcher and took him out the front door and into the ambulance. Our house became eerily quiet as I answered questions for a police officer. I tried to answer politely, though inside I was screaming to change out of my nightgown and follow the ambulance.

Before leaving for the hospital, I ran upstairs to talk to our kids. The scene in the boys' room is forever seared into my memory: All six kids were huddled together on the carpet, shadowed by the darkness. Their arms were wrapped around each other, heads tucked down, and they were audibly crying: our seventeen-year-old daughter, who would soon start her senior year of high school with its decisions and milestones; the three middle boys just coming of age; our six-year-old son just beginning to form memories with his dad of fishing, shooting the .22, and trips to the hardware store; and our four-year-old littlest girl, who could not have understood how permanently life was changing that early morning.

Everything in me wanted to assure them their dad would be okay. But as the words formed in my mouth, I stopped, realizing I couldn't promise it. I did the only thing I could—I knelt with them on the carpet, put my arms around them, and prayed. Getting up to head to the hospital, I spoke the only promise I could: "I will be back. I will be back."

Driving to the hospital, I thought of my children—bewildered, frightened, huddled together as they prayed and cried—and I wept. The hospital is just a few miles away, but it was the longest drive I've ever taken. Dan's life—all of life as we knew it—hung in the balance. Still, I remember feeling God's strong presence with me as I drove, as if the Holy Spirit was carrying me to the hospital and what lay ahead.

A Covenant Complete

At the ER, I sensed right away things weren't good. I wanted to hear the rush of intense patient care and treatment going on.

But it was pin-drop quiet. I'd called my sister and a friend on the way to the hospital. My friend and her husband had been waiting for me when I arrived and now sat with me in the quiet. Before long, I was led to a room that I immediately recognized as a counseling room. I sensed what this room meant: On earlier ER visits, I'd seen others go into rooms like this and leave crying. Sure enough, an ER doctor soon arrived and gently told me they had tried everything but were unable to revive Dan.

There are no scripts for these moments in life. These kinds of moments aren't supposed to *be* in the script. My friend reached her arms around me as I sobbed into her shoulder. When a worker arrived with paperwork to sign, I asked to see Dan and was led back to a large room, where he lay serene and still. I bent to kiss him one last time, hot tears spilling over my cheeks.

This was the man I was supposed to do the rest of life with. He was a fun dad, the adventurous one. He had always stepped in to fix situations too hard for me, had always been there to rescue me, like when my van slid into a ditch with three toddlers strapped into car seats or when I got myself into a mess giving too many yeses. There would be no more rescues from him, and I surely had been unable to rescue him, to *rescue us*.

There are no scripts for these moments in life. These kinds of moments aren't supposed to be in the script.

I stood and gazed at him, willing myself to memorize every feature of the face I had loved since I was sixteen. Two decades earlier, I had excitedly slipped a wedding band on his finger. Now, in a mix of gut-searing pain and hazy shock, I slipped it off and left for home.

"The two will become one flesh," Genesis tells us. We were one flesh, all right, and it felt like I had been ripped clean in half with dangled threads hanging raw. Our hopes, dreams, arguments, make-ups, hurts, and celebrations had woven us into one. Every one of our disagreements, every time we opened up vulnerably, each tiny tolerance, every effort we made to understand one another had been arduous work, but it had slowly, slowly formed something beautiful and strong.

There had been such great vision for our marriage, so much purpose as we worked together to build our family, disciple our children, and help shape them as they grew. So many hopes and dreams for next week, next month, and what our lives might look like years down the road. Now it all lay scattered in shards around me. Tomorrow's plans, the family trip, next week's schedule, our family life as we knew it were all shredded, and all that was left was agony and deep despair.

I had cried out for mercy. Even after the doctor had pronounced him dead, I hoped and prayed God would bring Dan back. *You brought back Lazarus, and you can do this*, I'd begged. But God had not spared Dan. In two short hours, life took a turn I never saw coming.

When Deep Disappointment Comes

Since you're reading this book, your life has probably taken a turn you never saw coming, and you're battling the daily refrain that *this isn't the story you planned*. Life can dish out many kinds of loss. I'm so sorry for the one you're walking. And while I've had to navigate the death of my husband and parent children through grief, there are lots of ways a life can fracture.

Maybe you're grappling with grief after the death of a spouse, parent, or child, or the death of a baby you were never able to meet. Maybe a marriage you thought was rock solid has ended, and neither your efforts nor prayers could save it. Maybe you're still in a marriage making the best of a commitment you made, but there is precious little life in it. Maybe your life crumbled because of a diagnosis, and days are now counted by appointments and medications. Perhaps you've clung to a dream with countless whispered prayers, but the waiting has stretched long past your own timeline. Maybe it's been a financial implosion for you, the loss of your savings, hard work, and dreams.

This book is for all of us navigating the space between the life we desperately wanted and the life we're living. Later in this book, you'll find stories of other women who navigated their own shattering disappointments.

While disappointment is universal, not all disappointments pack the same kind of loss. Imagine a sliding scale with disappointments on one end that are small and affect only a fraction of our life—like not being invited to a gathering with friends or not getting an acceptance on the offer you made for a house. Though they sting for a short while, the rest of life is stable and good and we can sail on fairly easily.

At the other end are life-shattering disappointments, the kinds of unexpected losses that usher in a host of hard emotions and permanently change life as we know it. These disappointments affect our routines, our relationships, and our future. They pull us into a dark pit of sadness, regret, fear, and despair, and trigger questions like, How in the world can I navigate these emotions? How can I find my footing and move forward? Will life ever feel good again?

I've asked these questions. I've stared at the gaping edge of disappointment and hoped to make it to tomorrow . . . and the next day. Let me walk with you through your deep loss, like my friend who showed up at the hospital for me.

Lots of people survive deep loss and disappointment but stay stuck in bitterness, anger, or pessimism. They're never truly happy again because they believe life was unfair. But we want to flourish again. We want to find our way through the tidal waves of emotion and figure out how to navigate life as it is now. We have to learn to live where we are and, even more, to love where we are.

It sounds hard, doesn't it? But with God, it is not impossible. He says to us in Luke 1:37, "For nothing will be impossible with God" (NASB). What God promises, God will bring about in us and for us.

There is a way through your hardship and there is good again on the other side of deep hurt. You may be waking up to a life you never expected, never wanted, and honestly still can't fathom, but you can flourish again. *You will smile again.* This may not be the road you chose, but let me share the biblical hope and practical guidance that can help you find your footing here and move forward well.

1

This Is Too Hard. I Cannot Do This.

The helpless call to him, and he answers; he saves them from all their troubles.

Psalm 34:6 GNT

Be assured, if you walk with Him and look to Him, and expect help from Him, He will never fail you.

George Mueller

The soft chimes on my phone alarm sounded on the nightstand next to me. I opened my eyes long enough to find the phone, slide the alarm to snooze, and set it back down. For one blissful second, life felt good and normal. But just as quickly, the bleak reality of my life rushed in like a bad Groundhog Day, sinking my emotions and wrenching my heart with familiar pain. Despair flooded in along with dread of the day's to-do list. Like the day before and the day before that, my list was filled from top to bottom with way more things to do than I could get done. Hard things far outside my comfort zone were now my daily normal.

I need to get my feet to the floor, I coached my heart. *My kids need me not just to show up, but to parent well. They've lost one parent and they cannot lose another.* I pulled back the blankets and willed myself to start another day.

THIS IS TOO HARD. I CANNOT DO THIS.

Every morning for more than a year, I wrote that line at the top of my journal pages in all caps with a strident underline to highlight how I felt. It wasn't just the physical pain of grief and the constant ache of loss. That alone was intense enough. It was also the heavy and constant weight of decisions I now had to make by myself, angst over how our one-income family was going to make it, heartbreak over the grief my children were experiencing that I couldn't fix, and worry over a host of issues I now faced.

After Dan died, I never asked God why. I know that's a common response for people facing a devastating heartbreak, and I'm grateful I somehow skipped that step. But I sure had other questions, like *what now?* What in the world did the unfathomable future hold? How would this affect my four-year-old, who could not grasp the permanency of death and who cried every day for more than a year saying she missed her daddy? What impact would this have on my six-year-old son whose childhood innocence was gone? While he seemed to play happily with neighborhood friends by day, he still wanted to sleep in my bed each night, and his tears spilled freely when I tucked him in. How was I going to raise five boys who needed their dad to help make it through the teen years to manhood? What about my seventeen-year-old daughter grieving her hero dad, who had taught her to fish and surf, who had championed her dreams, who would never walk her down a church aisle? How could God fix eight broken hearts?

I was mired in a place that was too hard for me to handle.

Has anyone ever tried to console you with the line that God never gives us more than we can handle? I know people mean well when they say it, may even think it's true, but I talk to women every week in circumstances that are overwhelming. Just last week, one friend opened up about her years-long solitary struggle to keep her marriage together as her husband's mental health plummeted. Making sure he got to appointments, ensuring he got his medication, and encouraging him through the roller coaster of emotions and outbursts was hard enough, but she simultaneously juggled her work, managed their home, and raised two children through it all.

Another young friend just went through the unthinkable. As a mama of two healthy children, she was pregnant with her third. In the thirty-ninth week of a seemingly healthy pregnancy, she stopped feeling the baby move and called her doctor. Tests revealed her baby boy had died in utero. For the next few hours, she went through a grueling labor to deliver her fully developed stillborn baby, trying to wrap reasoning around the reality that she'd never tuck him into the car seat for a ride home, never see his smile, never hear him belly laugh.

When life gets hard, others tell us we just need to buck up and power through. But here's where you and I can exhale the burden of having to be more or find more strength in ourselves than we have to handle overwhelming circumstances, because the Bible affirms that God very much allows us to encounter circumstances that are too big for us. We rarely understand why, but we can begin to see that God has never and will never leave us to bear it alone.

Some of the stoutest characters in Scripture went through situations that were too hard for them.

The prophet Elijah found himself in circumstances too difficult to handle. He was a bold and faithful prophet in Israel during the time when King Ahab, the most wicked king ever to sit on Israel's throne, ruled. Ahab was a murderous and power-hungry king who married his equal—Jezebel, the daughter of a pagan priest-king of Baal. Together, Ahab and Jezebel killed off as many of God's prophets as they could and led Israel into flagrant worship of Baal and Asherah.

Elijah was no featherweight. He had tremendous mettle as he faced Ahab and prophesied three years of famine for Israel because of Ahab's evil. He showed great perseverance as he went into hiding for three years and depended on God to provide for him. He demonstrated great faith as he prayed and raised a widow's son back to life. And in the event Elijah is most known for, he powerfully challenged eight hundred prophets of Baal on the summit of Mount Carmel to prove whose god was the true God. The prophets of Baal built an altar and sacrificed a bull, and from morning to evening, they chanted, sang, cut themselves, and prayed for Baal to ignite the fire on the altar. Of course, their powerless idol couldn't come through.

But then Elijah built an altar to God, sacrificed a bull, and went above and beyond by drenching it with water three times till water formed a moat around the altar. When Elijah prayed, God immediately sent fire, consuming the sacrifice and leaving the moat bone dry. But Elijah wasn't done. Alone except for his servant, he prayed intensely seven times that God would break the drought in Israel and send rain, which God did. Then, filled with the power of God, Elijah tucked up his cloak and ran to Jezreel *ahead* of King Ahab's chariots—a distance between seventeen and thirty miles. Elijah was no featherweight indeed.

And yet, when Jezebel threatened to kill Elijah just days after he witnessed God's power on the mountain, 1 Kings 19 tells us Elijah ran for his life into the wilderness of Judah. There, sitting alone under a broom tree, Elijah prayed for his death. "I have had enough, LORD," he said. "Take my life" (1 Kings 19:4).

Elijah, the bold, brash man full of God's power, had come to a place where circumstances were too hard to handle. I can sense in his words the exhaustion of fighting too many battles, the pain of too much loneliness, the dread of too much danger, and the fear of too much unknown. If Elijah had been a journaler, I wonder if he would have written *This is too hard. I cannot do this.*

God never shook his head at Elijah with a *tsk, tsk, tsk.* He never rebuked Elijah for reaching a place of utter dependence. How did God respond? He sent his presence to be with Elijah. "The LORD said, 'Go out and stand on the mountain in the presence of the LORD, for the LORD is about to pass by'" (1 Kings 19:11). Elijah watched as a powerful wind came by, followed by an earthquake and then a fire, but God was in none of those. God's presence came in a gentle whisper. Hearing the kind whisper of God's presence, Elijah covered his face with his cloak and stood before the presence of God.

When circumstances were too much for Elijah to handle, God answered with himself.

God allowed Elijah to endure circumstances too hard for him to handle, and he allows the same for us. It's not because our faith is too small, but that circumstances in a fallen world can simply become too difficult. Getting to the end of ourselves is where we become utterly dependent on God. It's where I found myself after Dan's death and where you may find yourself right now. But in our stubbornness, we often do everything we can to resist it.

The Idols of Self-Sufficiency and Control

When we find ourselves in a place of utter dependence on God, it often reveals two big idols we've let prop up our life: self-sufficiency and control.

Let's take a look at self-sufficiency first. Most of becoming an adult is learning to become self-sufficient. On one hand, taking care of ourselves is a good thing. But self-sufficiency becomes an idol when we believe we are strong enough, smart enough, and resourceful enough to handle what life is throwing at us.

God is an accessory to lives we sculpt that don't require us to wake up each day desperate for him to do what we cannot. We like to be the ones standing in a place of strength and plenty, offering, "How can I pray for you?" But please don't let us be the ones in desperate need of prayer. Even when we have needs, we try to manage or cover them up as long as possible so we won't come to that place where we realize we are not enough.

We also crave the idol of control. It stems from our deep-seated need for security. We usurp control in our parenting, plans, work, and finances, creating a false sense of security. We plan our future and write it in permanent marker so we know where we're headed and how to get there.

And our culture cheers both self-sufficiency and self-control. We fall into a pattern of self-reliance without daily dependence on God. Take our daily bread, for example. We may ask for it in the Lord's Prayer, but we never really rely on God to get food to our table each day. Where generations before planted crops, then prayed and trusted like crazy for the right conditions for seeds to grow and bear fruit, we've got grocery stores, restaurants, online ordering, and front-door delivery.

Yes, we've become a much more self-sufficient society. Advances in health care, for example, make us more self-sufficient.

Over-the-counter medications can take care of conditions that might have meant certain death in the past. When the car battery doesn't start or we walk out to a flat tire, we can call AAA. When the air conditioning goes out in July and we have to get a new condenser, there's no need to pray for God to provide funds when we can simply swipe the credit card. We insure away catastrophic loss and often expect the government to step in for other problems.

Now, I've used all these modern resources, which can be prudent and good, so I'm not knocking them. But I also realize how these advances insulate us from daily dependence on God, perhaps like no other generation before. Truth is, we like it this way because it's more comfortable to be in charge of the solution, to be independent and self-sufficient, rather than trust God for things we cannot fix.

Self-sufficiency and control are two words that signal idols at work in our life. I know; I've been there too. The idol of self-sufficiency is depending on my own strength and resources rather than depending on God. The idol of control is managing my life, agenda, and future rather than trusting God with my plans and decisions.

Circumstances that are too much for us to handle make us face the reality that self-sufficiency and control are illusions.

Circumstances that are too much for us to handle make us face the reality that self-sufficiency and control are illusions. Finding ourselves neck-deep in overwhelming, unexpected circumstances may be the first time we realize we are utterly dependent on God, which is partially why these crises are so shocking. How do we move beyond these centers of self and control and allow God to hold us in our deep loss and sadness? Let's go there.

Utterly Dependent on God

Proverbs 3:5–6 says to "trust in the Lord with **all your heart** and lean not on your own understanding; in **all your ways** submit to him, and he will make your paths straight" (emphasis added). You may know this verse—you may even have it memorized or framed in your home—but knowing this promise and standing on it when life is too much to handle are altogether different.

Most of us, if we're honest, only partially trust God. We want to trust him with all our heart, but we can handle what life throws at us most days. That's certainly been true for me. I can vividly see the picture my pastor created when I was eight years old of taking stick-figure me off the throne and placing God on the throne of my life. I wanted God to be Lord of my life then, and I've tried to make that so in the years since.

I've had seasons of needing to fully trust in God, like some tough financial periods Dan and I went through. But then life would right itself, and we weren't so needy anymore. Miscarriages, marriage issues, and parenting struggles have been hard places where I leaned on God. But as big as those struggles were at the time, it was as if I could wall off that part of life; I trusted God for that area, but the rest of life sailed on at a fairly normal rhythm. While I said I wanted to surrender fully, I really only surrendered on an as-needed basis. Maybe this feels true for you as well. And maybe you're not certain you really can trust God anymore.

We want control over our circumstances, our agendas, our finances, our family, and especially our future. We pray against the hard and worry that God might actually make us go through it. When we find ourselves in difficulty, we begin to wring our hands and pray not that God will glorify himself in it or that God will make us more Christlike through it, but that it will end. We want the hard parts fixed, and we want out as soon as possible. And while we might open one hand to God in trust because we have to, we keep the other tightly gripped around the rest of our life.

We push against the very thing that God wants from us: absolute surrender. As I wrote "This is too hard. I cannot do this," in my journal each day, another truth quietly presented itself: *Lisa, helpless dependence on God feels scary, but it is the best place to be.*

We were created for a relationship of complete dependence on God. Though we may hate the circumstances that get us there, finding ourselves totally surrendered to God is a coming home. We are, at last, where we were meant to be all along.

In that place of helpless dependence, I watched God do what I could not over and over again, and in such personal, practical ways. One of my biggest struggles was feeling overwhelmed with decisions. Ask any single parent: Decision fatigue is real. I was having to make umpteen decisions every day about the finances, house, kids, schooling, and more, all on my own. I'd never been good at decision-making, and now my mind felt muddled by a revolving door of dilemmas.

Helpless dependence on God feels scary, but it is the best place to be. We were created for a relationship of complete dependence on God.

But I wasn't alone; I began going to God for help. On one occasion, two of my teens asked to go on a ski retreat with a local Christian group. They'd been offered full scholarships, and while I knew this fun trip would brighten the heaviness they were feeling, my instinct was to say no because I didn't know the group well. But I promised to pray about it, and to my surprise, God gave a yes. After the leaders answered my questions, I trusted God knew better, held my breath, and told my kids they could go.

When I picked my daughter and son up after the weekend, they raved about how it was the best trip they'd been on—and they'd been on lots of youth trips! The leaders and other teens had been authentically welcoming and kind, the skiing a blast, and the Bible study deep and engaging. The more they gushed about the trip, the more I smiled in wonder. It was a stark reminder that my dependence on God was the best place to be.

I wish we had time and space for me to tell all the ways God practically and personally provided in my utter dependence on him. God delights in doing what we cannot. And while you wouldn't choose the circumstances that landed you here, you're now in a place to see God in ways you never would otherwise.

God Our Help

When we are utterly dependent on God, we get to see what he has declared all along: God is our help. Psalm 46:1 tells us God is "an ever-present help in trouble," and Psalm 124:8 says, "Our help is in the name of the Lord."

When we use the word *help*, we typically mean stepping in to aid or coming alongside to assist. God doesn't give a little support or assistance while we continue to control the situation. God offers divine help and covering over us, and as such, it is unlike anything we could ask for or imagine. His wisdom, his provision, his rescue, and his restoration are beyond what we can see and think.

In our desperate dependence, we know that if God doesn't act, we have no hope. And because we're completely surrendered, we find real hope in him.

I saw this as I studied Exodus 14 with my children. When God led the Israelites out of Egypt, he could have led them the short route straight toward the Promised Land. Instead, God took them the long way, where they found themselves trapped between the Red Sea and the Egyptian army. God intentionally put his beloved children in a place where they had no choice but to depend on him. And they saw God revealed as their Deliverer as they never would have known had they taken the shortcut. God met their need in a stunning and supernatural way when he parted the Red Sea and as he protected them against the Egyptian army with the pillar of fire.

As soon as the last Israelite foot touched dry ground, in a single swoop, God caused the Red Sea waters to flow back together, drowning the pursuing enemy. In that place of utter dependence, God readied Israel to declare without a shadow of doubt who God is and how he saves.

We need to let go of self-reliance for what C. H. Spurgeon calls "God-reliance."

> Fall back upon yourselves, lean upon your fellow creatures, trust upon earth-born confidences, and ye fall upon a rotten foundation that shall give way beneath you; but rest ye upon your God and upon your God alone, and the stars in heaven shall fight for you, yea, the stars in their courses, and things present and things to come, and heights, and depths, and all the creatures subservient to the will of the omnipotent Creator, shall work together for good to you, seeing that you love God and are depending upon his power.[1]

Oh, that we would trust God alone and know that he fights for us when we cannot. No matter what you're facing right now, no matter how overwhelmed you are or how impossible your circumstances look, "There is no one like the God of Israel. He rides across the heavens to help you, across the skies in majestic splendor" (Deuteronomy 33:26 NLT).

Friend, I know the circumstances that cause us to be helplessly dependent on God can be excruciating, but watch and listen: God is present with us when life feels out of control. Circumstances that are too hard to handle help us chisel out the idols of self-sufficiency and control and look to God alone.

The One who made your heart knows best how to mend it.

The One who shepherds your life knows best how to provide for you here.

And the One who holds your future knows best how to guide you there.

A Prayer for When Life Is Too Much to Handle

Dear Lord, how in the world can I navigate this circumstance? It is too much for me to handle, and I am overwhelmed. I look to you because you are my Rock when my world is rocking around me, and my Deliverer when I don't see a way through. I need you so desperately. And though it hurts like crazy, help me know that utter dependence on you is the best place to be. You see me and you have not left me alone. I trust you, even though I don't understand. In Jesus' name, amen.

2

Your Emotions Are Welcome Here

You've kept track of my every toss and turn through the sleepless nights, each tear entered in your ledger, each ache written in your book.

Psalm 56:8 *The Message*

There is a sacredness in tears. They are not the mark of weakness, but of power. They speak more eloquently than ten thousand tongues. They are the messengers of overwhelming grief, of deep contrition, and of unspeakable love.

Washington Irving

Jodi's world tumbled down around her. After months of hard counseling, countless prayers, weekly prayer walks, and a renewed commitment to her vows, she couldn't believe what she was hearing. Her husband's words shocked and stung to the core, shredding the hope she'd held and the victory she'd claimed over her marriage.

The pain felt like a sword plunged into her heart, forever dividing her life into two halves—before he left and after he left. She wanted to run to her bedroom, where she could cocoon in safety with her tears, but she remained frozen with fear, panic, and devastation. An unbearable heaviness settled over her, her family, and life as she knew it.

As hard as that moment was, there would come one that was worse. Having to tell her six- and ten-year-old sons their parents were divorcing and Dad would no longer live at the house was gut-wrenching. She watched her boys riding their bikes and laughing, unaware their childhood innocence was about to change forever. "I felt sick just thinking about the conversation we needed to have with them," Jodi recalled. "My stomach was in knots, and the pain intensified each time my kids scurried past me."

This was not the life she'd planned. She had imagined her boys' childhood anchored in an intact family and filled with unforgettable days like trips to Disneyland and hockey championships. This day would be unforgettable for her boys all right—the day they learned their family would forever split apart.

As she and her husband sat the boys down and calmly gave the news, her younger son burst into tears in Jodi's arms. Her older son did the opposite, outwardly showing no emotion, no tears, and no response. *We are completely screwing up our kids,* Jodi thought. *One day, they will be talking about this day with their therapist.* Jodi's heart broke all over again as hot tears flowed steadily down her cheeks.

Reeling from Hard Emotions

The emotions of life-altering loss are brutal. It takes enormous emotional, physical, mental, and spiritual space to process emotions like shock, sadness, despair, anger, fear, regret, confusion, vulnerability, and the like. These feelings are intense, they are persistent, and they are unpredictable.

When life falls apart, hard emotions cause us to feel like we're being crushed from the inside out. They consume our waking thoughts, mess with our daily routines, and prey on us in the nighttime hours as we struggle to sleep.

Where we once felt excited about weekend plans and house projects, Friday movie nights and school celebrations, we now feel numb. Nothing excites us anymore. Who cares if the house gets fixed up like we once dreamed? Who cares about the vacation we always wanted to take? Who cares about experimenting with heirloom tomatoes or trying new recipes in the kitchen? Life has changed forever, and with it, the things we loved about that life.

Before Dan's death, I'd describe myself as a believer, wife, mom, and homeschooling mama. At that point, I'd homeschooled for twelve years and I was all in. I loved planning, field-tripping, reading aloud late into the evening, and gathering with other families to teach. I pored over curriculum catalogs, led homeschool groups, started a debate club and a book club, and geeked out over things like the geography bee and the used-curriculum fair.

That all changed when Dan died. When new curriculum catalogs arrived in the mail, I tossed them without opening. While summer was normally a time of dreaming and planning for the next year, I worried I'd be able to teach at all. Dan had been the biggest supporter. He was my rescue on days I failed miserably, a sounding board when I was lost in the weeds, and he believed in me and our children. After he died, the delight of homeschooling drained like water from a tub, and I wondered if it would ever fill again.

The emotions that come with a serious life change surprise and unsettle us. We are left absolutely gutted, carrying the raw pain of loss throughout the day. Normal errands and routines are like a minefield of triggers that scream, *This is your life now!* Because most of us have never traveled the unexpected path we find ourselves on, the rush of negative emotions ushers in all kinds of worries. *Is it okay to feel like this? Shouldn't I be doing better by now? Will I ever feel better?*

At first, it's hard to get away from the intensity of these emotions. We wake in the morning, and for the briefest moment, life feels good and normal—and then *wham!* The despair, fear, and gloom fall heavier than an x-ray blanket. The ache stays with us as we move through the laundry and the car line, parenting and trying our best to get dinner on the table. We smile at the checkout counter and respond to polite small talk while our insides are aching. At night when the kids are in bed and our hands no longer have tasks to distract us from all we're missing and all we're facing, the stillness and quietness intensify the heavy emotions.

These hard, negative emotions are part of what make deep disappointment so brutal. I knew God would be faithful and I knew he would bring healing at some point, but I wanted to be healed, not *healing*. I wanted to fast-forward through the pain and the emotions that were pulling me under day after excruciating day.

But there is no fast-forwarding. There are no shortcuts through seasons of deep loss, and there is no bypassing the myriad hard emotions that come with them.

If we don't deal with hard emotions on our terms, they will come back on their terms later.

If we don't deal with hard emotions on our terms, they will come back on their terms later.

Stuffing our pain won't make it go away. Some days, I longed to escape the pain with a few days at Disney or the mountains or anywhere that would bring a jolt of fun. Alas, it's hard to push stop on schedules for seven kids, so I usually settled on binging Netflix.

Stuffing our pain will only make it pop up later, when we least expect it, and possibly when we're even more vulnerable. Stuffing emotions is like ignoring the warning light on the car's dash; after all, the car still runs, but just because it's running doesn't mean we aren't doing long-term damage. Similarly, the pain we ignore can return with deeper issues.

Masking pain won't make it disappear either. Pushing yourself to get on with life when you haven't fully grieved, or staying so busy that you simply don't have time to deal with the hard emotions, only delays the hard work needed to process the pain. Some people cover their pain with activities, shopping, or traveling for the adrenaline rush. But masking pain is as effective as painting over peeling wallpaper. Pain is ruthless and it demands attention.

I hate to even think about the destruction we bring on ourselves when we try to self-medicate the pain away. When life hurts that bad, self-medicating with alcohol, medications, food, shopping, or relationships is tempting. It may look like the answer to keep the intense pain at bay and help us feel good again, but at some point, that self-numbing wears off and reveals the pain that's still there, now compounded with a host of other issues.

The only way to deal with the hard emotions is to meet them head on and process through them.

And that's where it gets tricky, because when was the last time you welcomed your negative emotions? Most of us have been raised to get rid of our negative emotions. We've been taught it's not okay to walk around in a bad or sad mood. We're told to stop crying, we placate away a child's loneliness or frustration, and we stick a platitude across their disappointment. As a mom of seven, I see where I've done this in my own parenting. We do it because we think it's the best way to handle hard emotions—to maintain peace in our homes and make sure we're not deep-diving into messy, hard emotions. And so, most of us have learned to cry into the privacy of our pillows, to suck it up buttercup, and to will our way through sadness.

Our culture is good at celebrating the wins but not so much at mourning the losses.

So when life shatters like a Venetian glass vase and we're left with shards of pain, loneliness, sadness, disappointment, anger, and more—we don't know what to do with them or where to go.

Take every hard emotion to Jesus. We'll unpack what that looks like in the next chapter, but before we talk about how, let's agree that we don't have to fake or hide our emotions with Jesus. While you may want to fast-forward through hard emotions or avoid them altogether, you can be sure of this:

Jesus
welcomes
your
most difficult
emotions.

Jesus Welcomes Your Pain

While we may be uncomfortable with hard emotions, God is not. The God who created us also created our emotions.

I have to admit, this was a startling and late-to-the-table realization for me. After years and years of battling my emotions, trying to keep them at bay like they were the enemy, I realized that when God created us fearfully and wonderfully, it included our emotions as much as it included our organs and bones. We are made to think and do and *feel.*

We so often fall into the trap of thinking we can only present our perfect selves before God when the opposite is true. God tells us to come to him with our weariness and burdens. Come to him with our pain and despair. Come to him with our struggles and fear. God understands our difficult feelings, and he makes space for them.

Our hard emotions aren't signs that we're handling our hurt all wrong, but indicators we're responding to circumstances gone wrong.

Our hard emotions aren't signs that we're handling our hurt all wrong, but indicators we're responding to circumstances gone wrong.

Our emotions are not only safe with God, they are safest with God. Our emotions don't surprise God or put him off. Nor does he give us a timer for our pain. It's not our emotions that become issues but what we do with them. God intends for us to take every negative emotion to him. We don't have to stuff them or mask them or fake them. Instead, we can bring our most honest, gut-level, grueling emotions and lay them before God. I mean, he already knows them better than we ever will because he experienced them himself.

Jesus Understands Your Pain Because He Walked Your Pain

Jesus didn't insulate himself from difficult emotions. Scripture shows us Jesus experienced pain, anger,[1] anguish, oppression, rejection, sorrow,[2] weakness,[3] loneliness,[4] betrayal, and exhaustion.[5] Jesus left the glory of heaven, the perfection of fellowship with the Father and Holy Spirit, the beauty of undefiled worship and honor, to dwell with us on this messy, messed-up earth. Jesus not only took on human flesh, but human emotions as well.

He experienced devastating loss to the point of tears when Lazarus became sick and died (John 11). Lazarus and his sisters, Martha and Mary, were close friends of Jesus; he often stayed in their home. The sisters had sent word to Jesus that Lazarus was critically ill, and yet instead of immediately going to him, Jesus intentionally waited two days. By the time Jesus reached their home, Lazarus had been buried for four days.

As Jesus arrived, Mary fell at his feet. You can hear the emotion in her words: "Lord, if you had been here, my brother would not have died" (John 11:32).

Have you ever said something like that to God? *Lord, things would look so different if you had only*______________. Mary was reeling from deep disappointment, and do not miss that she took it straight to Christ. She must have felt safe to express her raw emotion to him. But Jesus didn't rebuke her or dismiss her emotion; he welcomed it with the tenderest of responses.

"When Jesus saw her weeping, and the Jews who had come along with her also weeping, he was deeply moved in spirit and troubled" (John 11:33). Jesus asked where they had buried Lazarus, and they told him to come and see. And then the Bible gives this short and powerful verse: "Jesus wept" (John 11:35).

Unlike the loud public wailing of the mourners following Mary and Martha, John records that Jesus *dakruó*, a Greek word that means to shed silent tears or weep quietly.[6] Jesus was deeply moved by Martha's and Mary's pain. Jesus was about to raise Lazarus, yet before he ever changed the circumstance, he entered their grief.

Jesus also experienced agonizing emotions the night before his crucifixion in the garden of Gethsemane. As Jesus prayed for God to take the cup of suffering from him, he became sorrowful and deeply distressed.

Hebrews describes Jesus' emotion in the garden that night with color: "In the days of his flesh, Jesus offered up prayers and supplications, with loud cries and tears, to him who was able to save him from death" (Hebrews 5:7 ESV). HELPS Word-studies defines the Greek word for *cries* as "loud crying, done with pathos (great emotion); clamorous screaming (shrieking) that is extremely boisterous, like a wounded person emitting 'unearthly' (non-human) types of sounds."[7]

This was not a one-Kleenex kind of sniffle. This was a hand-me-the-whole-box, all-out guttural cry that came from the deepest, rawest emotion.

Jesus gets our hard emotions. God welcomes our emotions because he created them and experienced them.

Most of the time, I brought my hard emotions to God while alone with my Bible, but there were a few whole-box-of-tissues days. One day, I could sense the kids felt as heavy as I did, so after lunch I called off homeschooling. We headed to Target so they could spend gift cards they'd received, thinking it would be good medicine for all of us. On the way home, traffic came to a crawl because of a wreck, and as we got closer, I saw the wreck involved my other car! My daughter and son had been driving home from class, and the totaled car now held up four congested lanes.

I pulled over and, after making sure my daughter and son weren't injured, I took care of details with the police officer, the insurance company, and the other two drivers. As the tow truck hauled off the car, I came undone. Months of trying to hold everything together for my kids, our home, our finances, our life was too much, and I broke. While my kids had seen me cry softly before, they now saw me audibly crying as I drove home through a blur of tears.

"Cereal for dinner," I announced at home, heading straight for my bedroom. Falling onto my bed, I muffled audible cries I could no longer control with my pillow and eventually fell asleep completely spent.

Listen, friend, if no one around you understands your pain, loneliness, exhaustion, sadness, or despair—God does. He understands it, he has experienced it, and he always invites you to take your emotion to him.

Never Apologize for the Tears God Created

Who knew a body could cry so many tears? I mean, I've had days when I just needed a good cry, and I've shed my share of tears over a sappy movie or tearjerker book ending. But I had never experienced the weeks and months of daily tears that spilled so regularly after Dan died.

Sometimes they were tears of plain-out missing him. Sometimes they were tears of longing for what would never be again and realizing afresh all that would never come to be. Sometimes they were tears of frustration at having to tackle one more new thing, and sometimes they were tears at God's goodness right in the midst of the hard.

When life implodes in loss, it's like a valve is opened and our tears flow freely throughout the day. I cried at triggered memories, I cried while praying, I cried while running and thinking about all I was facing. I cried over coffee when friends asked how I was doing, I cried while talking with my kids through their struggles, and I cried pretty much every morning while doing my Bible time alone in my car. I cried myself to sleep and I cried in my dreams. On Sundays, worship undid me. The song set seemed hand-selected for me, every phrase unleashing the deepest worries and prayers of my shattered heart. There, wrapped in the presence of God, my messy mix of emotions triggered hot tears for all that was lost and the hope for what God had for me.

I was glad for the dim lights during worship that hid my tears. I often found myself apologizing for my tears when I was with others. One kind man at church lent me no fewer than three handkerchiefs on different occasions because I always seemed to break into tears when I least expected it. I'd apologize for my tears when they came in conversation with a friend, with my parents when I was relaying a story or a concern, and embarrassingly in conversations with people I didn't even know.

One day in my writing, I chased down some research on our tears. I was stunned to see how unique and beneficial they are. That day, I decided I'd no longer apologize for tears. God gave us a huge gift when he gave us tears. Of all the creatures he made, he gave humans alone the release of emotional tears.[8] And God gave us tears not just to express deep feelings, but also to help us physically and emotionally process the pain behind them.

Tears are a kindness from a loving God who never expects us to get through things too big to handle on our own. Science now backs up the incredible benefits of emotional tears in three key ways.

Tears release stress. The chemical makeup of our emotional tears—the tears that come from sadness, disappointment, loss, and even anger—is completely different from tears that keep our eyes lubricated as we blink, or tears from irritants like dust or cutting an onion. Lubricating tears are 98 percent water while emotional tears are filled with stress hormones and toxins.[9] Emotional tears carry those toxins and stress hormones out of our body—a literal outlet for stress.

Tears calm us. Emotional crying lowers the heart rate and blood pressure. It helps to settle our physical stress responses and bring a sense of calm.[10] You've probably experienced how having a good cry releases pent-up stress and emotion and feels so cathartic afterward.

Tears soften the pain. When we cry, our body releases endorphins.[11] Endorphins are often called feel-good hormones, and they work two ways: They reduce the negative feelings of pain while increasing the positive feelings of pleasure. Endorphins provide a physical buffer to pain.

What kindness God built into the details of his design for us. You never have to apologize for your tears or wish them away. They are a gift to help your body process difficult experiences.

Not one of your teardrops escapes God's attention. Psalm 56:8 NLT says, "You keep track of all my sorrows. You have collected all my tears in your bottle. You have recorded each one in your book."

God cares about you so tenderly that he knows every single tear you've cried, and more than that, he's recorded it for all eternity. Every tear of hurt, betrayal, longing, grief, or frustration you cry is noticed by God. Your tears matter. When our heart is shattered and life is upended, we don't have a God who stays far off. He knows the tiniest details of our pain and grief.

Our tears may seem endless, but they are not the end of the story. Our despair and brokenness, pain and loss are not cul-de-sacs where we will keep circling forever. We may cry more than we ever thought possible, but it won't always feel like this.

God is a restoring God and an abundant-life God. He delights in bringing beauty from ashes and gladness from grief. Psalm 126:5–6 says, "Those who sow with tears will reap with songs of joy. Those who go out weeping, carrying seed to sow, will return with songs of joy, carrying sheaves with them." If we do the hard work of processing our emotions—without stuffing them, masking them, or self-medicating them—our hard emotions will begin to soften.

God has given us tears as part of his comfort. He not only collects them in a bottle, he redeems them.

A Prayer for Hard Emotions

Oh, God, I can barely put words to this prayer. My tears have been my food night and day. My heart is crushed and I am broken. How did I get here? Life feels heavy and dark, and my soul is in anguish. This is not what I wanted, Lord. It feels like I've been overlooked and forgotten. But I know darkness is not dark to you and that you hem me in behind and before. You have laid your hand on me. So I put my hope in you. You are worthy, and in this storm, I choose to trust you. In Jesus' name, amen.

3

The Great Exchange

> If your law had not been my delight, I would have perished in my affliction.
>
> Psalm 119:92

> Within the Scripture there is balm for every wound, a salve for every sore.
>
> C. H. Spurgeon

The problem isn't our hard emotions. The problem is that our hard emotions can fuel lies.

We saw in the last chapter that God welcomes our most raw and real emotions. And while our emotions are valid, they aren't always reasonable. Feelings do a good job of signaling when we're in pain, but they do a bad job of telling us the truth in that pain.

See if you can identify with any of these emotion-fueled lies:

- The good life is over; everything I could ever want is behind me.
- I'm not worthy of being loved.
- God is withholding good from me but giving it to everyone else.
- I'm all alone in this.
- My future is a bleak black hole.
- There's no way out of this.
- My heart will never stop aching; it will always feel like this.
- God will never be able to use me again.
- The other shoe is going to drop at any moment.
- My relationships, my family, and my memories are all based on lies.
- I could have done more; I should have known; I could have changed the outcome.
- I can't move forward and leave what I loved behind.
- I'm too old/too unlovable/too scarred to feel beautiful and happy again.

Not only do our emotions conjure lies, but they also fluctuate. Rather than march us forward on a linear path toward wholeness, they vacillate wildly. They ebb and flow, rise and fall, hit hard and linger deep. Just when we think we've made huge strides through the darkest emotions, we find ourselves in another pit with lies taunting us that we'll never make it through.

If God created us with emotions, surely he has a way for us to move forward through them. And he does. We have to anchor our fickle feelings and the lies they foment in God's unchanging truth.

The Great Exchange

A run will do me some good, I thought, lacing up my running shoes. I had so much angst bottled up in me, and I needed to get it out. But as soon as my feet hit the familiar paved trail, my worry went into overdrive. The longer I ran, the higher my anxiety rose. I was up to my eyeballs in decisions of all kinds—estate issues, financial questions, homeschool needs, and house upkeep, along with decisions as I single-parented a preschooler, kindergartner, tweens, teens, and my oldest in college. I'd never liked making decisions, and now the one person I most needed to talk things through with was gone. It felt like too much to unload on any one friend, so I ran with it all mixed in a brooding concoction of worry, fear, and despair.

Like a shaken two-liter bottle of soda, it reached a pressure point inside my head. Overwhelmed by it all, I stopped running and, alone on that trail, my words tumbled out audibly to God.

"Lord, I need you to guide me clearly," I pleaded, my tears mixing with sweat. "I cannot figure this all out. I need you to clearly lead me like the pillar of fire and the pillar of cloud. I know you can do it. You did it for the Israelites and I need it now for me."

It was the unrestrained prayer of a woman desperate for God's help. I'm not sure what I expected. I hadn't planned this prayer. It was simply the release of my overburdened heart and mind, like uncapping that shaken two-liter bottle. No sooner were the words out of my mouth than I heard distinctly in my spirit, *You stay in my Word and I will lead you.*

You better believe I took God up on it. I mean, in one sense, this wasn't news to me. I know God speaks to us through Scripture.[1] I'd done Bible studies for years and I had a stack of devotionals on my bedside table, but I tended to be a fair-weather

Bible study girl. Through college and as a young mom, I'd joined Bible studies and grown spiritually by leaps and bounds, and when I wasn't in a formal Bible study group, I tried to read the Bible on my own. But I often picked my Bible up out of a sense of duty, to catch up on Bible study homework or because I had to prepare a Sunday lesson for my middle school girls.

Now, catapulted into a life I didn't expect or want, my time in the Bible was completely different. I no longer opened my Bible out of obligation but out of desperation. I needed God's Word more than I needed food. Getting into God's Word became my first focus each day because it was there I found the strength and hope I needed. So began a new daily rhythm for me. Each morning, I'd get my kids up and going on breakfast, chores, and schoolwork, and then I'd head out by myself to that same park where I'd begged God to guide me. There was nothing magical about this little park; it was simply a close, quiet spot where I could be alone without interruptions from my kids or distractions in the house.

Some people have a prayer closet. I have a minivan. Each morning, I opened my journal, turned to a fresh page, and poured out all that was on my heart. Sometimes it was a concern I had for a particular child and my quandary of how in the world to parent through it. Some days, I worried how we were going to survive financially, or I felt paralyzed by another new task that seemed too foreign and too hard. Other days, I was exhausted just thinking about my growing must-do list. And always, always I poured out the grueling emotions threatening to pull me under altogether. I journaled my questions, my worries, and my needs. It was an ongoing conversation with God, sometimes through audible words and tears, sometimes through pen on paper.

Then, closing my journal, I opened my Bible for that day's reading. I didn't go looking for verses I thought might apply to me or let my Bible providentially fall open to a passage. Our church had been reading through the Bible in a year,[2] and though the year was halfway over, I joined in, beginning with that day's reading.

And that's when it happened.

Morning after morning, in the front seat of my Sienna minivan, a holy exchange took place. This ordinary mom with overwhelming need met with the God of the universe, laid down her burdens, and picked up his grace.

I learned a remarkable truth: We can give God our pain, despair, fear, doubt, sadness, and questions, and he will give us his hope, strength, love, truth, and life through the pages of Scripture. It didn't matter whether I was reading in the dense passages of Leviticus or the poetic praises of Psalms, God always spoke straight to me, affirming who he is and how faithful he is.

It's what I've come to call the Great Exchange. Daily, we can go to God with our brokenness and draw strength from his Word. We can exchange our worry for God's peace, our despair for his hope, our pain for his promise, and the lies for his truth.

Nothing calms us, grounds us, lifts our head, chisels our heart, fixes our perspective, renews our hope, confirms our purpose, restores our soul, and woos us like the Word of God.

We can exchange our worry for God's peace, our despair for his hope, our pain for his promise, and the lies for his truth.

The Great Exchange allows us to lay every difficult emotion, every painful memory, every hard struggle, every fear we're facing, and every overwhelming task at the throne of grace and receive God's eternal, soul-satisfying, heart-mending, life-giving, hope-filled, active, and powerful Word that penetrates the deepest places of our soul. In complete safety, we can lay bare before God what we sometimes can't even put to words.

As I went to God for this Great Exchange each morning, I received enough hope to go back home, parent my children, and take care of the tasks for that day. But it wasn't enough for the whole week. Like the manna God rained down each day in the wilderness, I had to go back to God the next day for more. It's not just an exchange; it's a daily exchange.

A Daily Dose of Hope

When God led the Israelites out of Egypt, he led them to the wilderness, where they found themselves without water or food. Think of it—more than a million men, women, children, nursing mamas, elderly, and growing teenage boys without food or water. God intentionally led them to a place of utter need where they were completely dependent on him. Sound familiar? Let's drop in on the Israelites moaning and groaning about their hunger in Exodus 16:

> In the desert the whole community grumbled against Moses and Aaron. The Israelites said to them, "If only we had died by the LORD's hand in Egypt! There we sat around pots and meat and ate all the food we wanted, but you have brought us out into this desert to starve this entire assembly to death."
>
> Then the LORD said to Moses, "I will rain down bread from heaven for you. The people are to go out each day and gather enough for that day. In this way I will test them and see whether they will follow my instructions. . . . In the morning you will be filled with bread. Then you will know that I am the LORD your God."
>
> Exodus 16:2–4, 12

Sure enough, each morning the Israelites found white flakes like frost covering the desert. They had never seen it before and called it *manna*, a Hebrew word meaning "what is this?" or "whatness."[3] "Moses said to them, 'It is the bread the Lord has given you to eat. This is what the Lord has commanded: Everyone is to gather as much as they need'" (Exodus 16:15–16).

Morning after morning, for forty years, the Israelites woke up to fresh manna in the wilderness (except Saturdays, since the double portion gathered on Fridays lasted through the Sabbath). God wasn't just providing food for Israel. He could have done that by leading them to orchards, fields, and flocks they could manage themselves for forty years. God provided a table in the wilderness, set with enough sustenance for that day. Morning in and morning out, they learned daily dependence on God.

Let's look at three key principles from God's provision of manna. First, they had to gather it; it didn't land at their tent doors. Each family had to go out and gather food for that day. Second, it was from the hand of God; they couldn't get this anywhere else. It wasn't something they could produce or grow themselves. Third, it was fully sufficient for each person's need. Working man, pregnant mama, toddler, or growing teen, God supernaturally made what they gathered perfectly sufficient. Their job was to gather manna; God saw to it that their needs were fully satisfied.

As they woke each morning to fresh manna, gathered their daily portion, and ate it, God revealed more than the truth that he will supply all of our needs. Deuteronomy 8:3 says, "Yes, he humbled you by letting you go hungry and then feeding you with manna, a food previously unknown to you and your ancestors. **He did it to teach you that people do not live**

by bread alone; rather, we live by every word that comes from the mouth of the LORD" (NLT, emphasis added).

Just as God provided daily bread to feed Israel physically, God provides his Word to feed us spiritually. God's Word is to our spirit what bread is to our body.

Like the Israelites, we must gather our daily Word from God. Whether we do it on an app or with a physical Bible, we need to open it, read it, study it, and meditate on it. It won't just land on our doorstep.

God's Word is to our spirit what bread is to our body.

And like the manna that came exclusively from God, we can't meet our spiritual need anywhere else. We can't shop for it, find it on a dating site, binge it on Netflix, or get it from friends or family. Only God can meet our spiritual need.

We can trust that God's Word is always fully sufficient to meet our need. That's the beauty of the Great Exchange. We bring God our brokenness, our inability, our weakness, our lack, and our utter need, and God comforts us, equips us, builds us up, guides us, warns us, strengthens us, anchors us, brings us hope, gives us wisdom, sets us free, and restores our joy, meeting our specific spiritual need on that particular day.

Making the Great Exchange a daily exchange is key to processing hard emotions. I certainly had times when my day got ahead of me or I put off Bible study for days because I was taking care of other things. But before I knew it, my emotions would plummet and I'd realize I'd drifted from the anchor of God's Word. We need a daily exchange—of our thoughts for God's thoughts—and a reminder of his promises, his character, and his hope.

What if you're so angry or upset you don't feel like turning to God? I asked that question recently on my Facebook page and received dozens of responses, like this one from Julie: "I'll never forget one time I was very angry and disappointed about my circumstances. . . . I knew I was wrong but I just wanted to wallow in my self-pity, when the Holy Spirit told me to pray. I did not want to!" Julie's prayer was raw and real as she unpacked her ugly thoughts and hard emotions before God.

Julie says that while her circumstance didn't immediately change, she felt God's presence. "He gave me peace that he wanted my honest response, which was crying out to him in a moment of anger and disbelief rather than not letting him in at all."

Julie's raw prayer and what I found in my own daily exchange have a long history: The Bible calls it *lament*.

Letting Lament Help You Process Emotions

Lament is the biblical practice of bringing our hard emotions to God and renewing our hope in his character and promises. Lament frees us from carrying the unbearable weight of our painful emotions alone.

Lament, says Esther Fleece in her book *No More Faking Fine*, is saying, "God I'm hurting, will you meet me here? And as such it is a prayer God always answers."[4] Esther says God "wants pain to leave our hearts, minds, and bodies but He doesn't expect it to happen overnight, nor does He give us a formula for healing. But He does give us a language, and that language is lament."[5]

Lament shows up as quiet tears, audible cries, choking sobs, strident anger, and "groanings too deep for words."[6] Lament is voicing your hardest emotions and questions to God, leaving them there, and choosing to trust God's comfort and faithfulness.

"Lament is a prayer in pain that leads to trust," says Mark Vroegop. Though lament starts with hard emotions and hard questions, it never stays there. It's "a path to praise as we are led through our brokenness and disappointment. . . . It's the path from heartbreak to hope."[7]

The language of lament is in multiple books of the Bible but shows up in full color in the Psalms. Look at the following passages and note how the psalmist expresses raw emotions and asks hard questions and then chooses to trust God's faithfulness.

The emotion: "I am worn out from sobbing. All night I flood my bed with weeping, drenching it with my tears."

The trust: "Go away, all you who do evil, for the LORD has heard my weeping. The LORD has heard my plea; the LORD will answer my prayer" (Psalm 6:6, 8–9 NLT).

The emotion: "How long, LORD? Will you forget me forever? How long will you hide your face from me? How long must I wrestle with my thoughts and day after day have sorrow in my heart? How long will my enemy triumph over me?"

The trust: "But I trust in your unfailing love; my heart rejoices in your salvation. I will sing the LORD's praise, for he has been good to me" (Psalm 13:1–2, 5–6).

The emotion: "Have mercy on me, LORD, because I'm depressed. My vision fails because of my grief, as do my spirit and my body. My life is consumed with sadness; my years are consumed with groaning. Strength fails me because of my suffering; my bones dry up."

The trust: "But me? I trust you, LORD! I affirm, 'You are my God.' . . . All you who wait for the LORD, be strong and let your heart take courage" (Psalm 31:9–10, 14, 24 CEB).

> **The emotion:** "Save me, O God! For the waters have come up to my neck. . . . I am weary with my crying out; my throat is parched. My eyes grow dim with waiting for my God."
>
> **The trust:** "But as for me, my prayer is to you, O LORD. . . . In the abundance of your steadfast love answer me in your saving faithfulness. . . . For the LORD hears the needy and does not despise his own people who are prisoners" (Psalm 69:1, 3, 13, 33 ESV).

Bringing our raw emotions to God is the first step of processing our pain, but then we have a choice. We can sit and stew in them, or we can trust that God knows what he's doing, he will bring us through, and life will be good again. Let's look at this difference in the lives of two women who had similar losses but chose to process their emotions differently.

Lament Is Not Complaint: Naomi and Ruth

The story of Ruth and Naomi may be very familiar to you, but for now, push pause on what you already know and let's look for fresh application for processing our emotions.

The story of these two women, found in Ruth, goes like this: Naomi (whose name means "Pleasant") married Elimelek (whose name means "My God Is King") in Ephrathah (a name for Bethlehem meaning "fruitfulness"). So, we have Pleasant marrying My God Is King in the village of Fruitfulness. Life started out well, and I imagine, like most young wives, Naomi dreamed of a happily-ever-after life.

Naomi and Elimelek had two sons, but then life took several hard turns. First, because of a famine, they moved to Moab. Next, Elimelek died, leaving Naomi a widow. Her two boys married Moabite women, and then the unthinkable happened: both sons died. Naomi was now a childless widow, navigating a life she couldn't have seen coming.

Hearing the famine was over, Naomi decided to return to Bethlehem with her daughters-in-law, but on the way, urged them instead to return to their families. "Why would you come with me? Am I going to have any more sons, who could become your husbands? . . . No, my daughters. It is more bitter for me than for you, because the LORD's hand has turned against me!" (Ruth 1:11, 13).

Naomi had lost faith in God and his goodness and thought it was better to send Orpah and Ruth back to their Moabite families than to go forward with God. Orpah turned back, but Ruth refused, promising she'd never leave Naomi alone. "Where you go I will go, and where you stay I will stay. Your people will be my people and your God my God" (Ruth 1:16). As Ruth and Naomi entered Bethlehem, the whole town was abuzz. "Could this be Naomi?" the village women asked.

But look at Naomi's response. "Don't call me Naomi [Pleasant]," she told them. "Call me Mara [Bitter], because the Almighty has made my life very bitter. I went away full, but the LORD has brought me back empty. Why call me Naomi? The LORD has afflicted me; the Almighty has brought misfortune upon me" (Ruth 1:20–21).

I feel for Naomi. She had suffered catastrophic loss. But she let her circumstances turn her from trusting God. She stewed in her loss, becoming bitter and blaming God. She bought the lie that everything good was behind her and it was all God's fault.

Ruth had also suffered losses. She too was a childless widow, and while Naomi was returning to her home and family, Ruth was leaving hers. Though she must have grieved, Scripture never records Ruth holding her losses against God.

There is a difference between grieving what's lost and grumbling over what's lost. In grief, we cry out to God; in grumbling, we cry out against him.

Naomi took her raw emotions to God but cried out against him. She gave in to the lies that God wasn't for her, the good life was all behind her, there was no hope for her future, and she could never be happy again. When her feelings screamed, "*I feel awful!*" she embraced a false corollary that life was awful and would always be awful.

We have a choice with our hard emotions: buy in to the lies and grumble against God, or exchange the lies for truth and trust God.

Grumbling says, I deserve different. God is against me.

Lament says, I wish this was different, but I trust God is for me.

Our emotions only tell us about the pain of the moment; they cannot tell us the truth of our future.

The truth for Naomi and Ruth was the famine was over. The truth was Naomi had a home, a family, and a community to come back to. The truth was the spring harvest was in, signaling winter had passed. It was a time of new beginnings and new life, of joy and thanksgiving to God for his goodness.

Our emotions only tell us about the pain of the moment; they cannot predict the future.

Naomi had suffered unexpected loss, but she had also experienced unexpected gain. She had the love and help of her loyal daughter-in-law, Ruth, who had promised to stay with Naomi not just until Naomi got on her feet, but for Naomi's entire life. Her bitterness caused her to miss something else: Ruth's new faith. On that road to Bethlehem, Ruth not only gave her heart to follow Naomi, but gave her heart to follow God as well.

If Naomi had turned to God instead of grumbling against him, I wonder if her eyes would have been opened to see how God was working for her.

We don't always get to choose our circumstance, but we can always choose our response. We can either cry out *to* God—a prayer that draws us to God and lets God carry us through our hard emotions—or we can cry out *against* God—casting blame that turns us from him, leads to bitterness, and heaps even more weight onto the hard emotions we're already carrying.

Every time we're hit by a hard emotion, we face this choice. Every time our heart questions, *How long?* or *Why this?* or *How could you?* we have a choice: cry out to God or cry out against God.

Pain doesn't get the final say in your story. God does.

In the midst of Naomi's and Ruth's pain, God was already working in ways they could not begin to imagine. Maybe you know the end of their story.

Through God's providential hand, Ruth married Boaz—a godly distant relative of Elimelek—and had a son, who was "a restorer of life."

That little boy was more than life to Naomi and Ruth. That little boy was Obed, the grandfather of King David. That's right, Naomi became the great-great-grandmother of Israel's renowned king, the giant slayer, the man after God's own heart, and the royal line through which God would bring his Son Jesus.

If Naomi had known the good God had planned for her, a future that far exceeded what she could have asked for or imagined, would she have been bitter? Would she have demanded different? In the midst of Naomi's loss—and Ruth's—God was working to bring about their deliverance. And not only deliverance for them, but all mankind.

Your hard emotions cannot tell you the end of your story. Your hard questions cannot answer how God is working.

As we lament loss, let's choose to trust that God knows what he is doing and that he is working his purpose even if we can't yet see it.

Because one day, if we keep doing the hard work of taking our emotions to God and trusting, we will be able to tell the whole story.

A story of brutal loss and beautiful restoration.

A story of unexpected emptiness and unimagined fullness.

A story of earthly pain and eternal purpose.

A Prayer to Exchange Feelings for Truth

Heavenly Father, thank you for your enduring Word. Give me a love and thirst for your Word that nothing else will satisfy. I open wide my mouth so that you can fill it. Draw me to you daily, and feed me so I can walk this difficult season. Help me anchor in your truth, not in my feelings or my circumstances. I choose to trust you even though I don't understand. I want to know you more, to see you revealed in Scripture, and to love you with my whole heart, soul, mind, and strength. May my heart be good soil ready to receive what you teach, and to align my will to yours. In Jesus' name, amen.

4

Find Your Footing

> You know with all your heart and soul that not one of all the good promises the LORD your God gave you has failed. Every promise has been fulfilled; not one has failed.
>
> Joshua 23:14

> When a train goes through a tunnel and it gets dark, you don't throw away the ticket and jump off. You sit still and trust the engineer.
>
> Corrie ten Boom

It's easy enough to say that God is faithful. I mean, we stamp it on our coffee mugs, stitch in onto T-shirts, and sing about it on Sundays. I've taught my kids about God's faithfulness since they were babies, through stories, songs, and Bible verses. I'd seen his faithfulness in my own life and the lives of my friends and family. Of course we believe God is faithful. It's a central tenet of the Christian faith, and if we say we follow Jesus, it's a belief we squared away a long time ago.

Or at least we *think* we squared it away. Because truth is, it's one thing to declare God's faithfulness when life is going as planned, and something else altogether when those plans shatter without notice. God's faithfulness goes without saying, but it does not go without testing.

The tension is not so much a lofty theological quandary of whether God is faithful, but whether God will be faithful *in this, to me.*

After Dan died, one of my chief worries was raising my children as a single mom. Parenting was tough enough when I had Dan to lean on for decisions, and I could count on his strengths to balance my shortcomings. Now God's promises to give wisdom, to guide, and to be strength in my weakness were put to the test in my solo parenting.

But we cannot find our footing in the unexpected, much less move forward into a future we never saw coming, unless we know God will be faithful no matter what. If we don't nail this down now, we will be paralyzed by fear and unable to take steps forward when life doesn't look the way we thought it would.

What if we could settle the question of God's faithfulness once and for all? What if we didn't have to revisit the question of God's faithfulness every time we encountered something new or too hard for us? This is possible for us when we cinch our doubts in three areas. To do that, we need to see what the gospel teaches us about God's faithfulness, then what God's faithfulness actually means, and finally, what exactly God has promised us.

First, the gospel. It's the entire reason I'm writing this book, and maybe the reason you're reading it. If not for the gospel, we would have zero hope for life on this earth or life after death. God did not just leave us down here, helpless in our suffering. In his unimaginable love, God sent his only Son to live with us, to die in our place for our wrongdoing, and through Jesus' resurrection, to give us eternal life when we trust God in faith.

Maybe, like me, you believe that. But here's where the gospel challenged me: If I trust God for my eternal life after death, why am I not also trusting him for every earthly need?

That was the question that stopped me short a few weeks after Dan died. I was alone in my car and found myself in a familiar cycle of worry. My mind was swirling with a fretful mix of emotions, and I was overwhelmed at the tasks on my plate and all the unknown that lay ahead.

Idling at a stoplight, a familiar Bible story came to me. It was the account of the paralyzed man whose four friends lowered him through the roof to the feet of Jesus. Luke 5 tells us Jesus was teaching in a house so full, the friends couldn't get in. So they went to the roof, cut a hole, and lowered their friend to the ground right in front of Jesus and the gathered crowd. While the friends had brought the man for physical healing, to the astonishment of the scribes and Pharisees in the room, Jesus told the paralyzed man his sins were forgiven.

Forgive sins? the religious leaders thought. *Only God can forgive sins*, and immediately the scribes and Pharisees silently accused Jesus of blasphemy. They didn't need to say it out loud; Jesus knew exactly what they were thinking, and his response is key: "'Which is easier: to say, "Your sins are forgiven," or to say, "Get up and walk?" But I want you to know that the Son of Man has authority on earth to forgive sins.' So he said to the paralyzed man, 'I tell you, get up, take your mat and go home'" (Luke 5:23–24).

The paralyzed man did just that. He stood up, grabbed his mat, and headed home to the amazement of everyone in the house.

Jesus was showing he not only had authority over physical healing, but spiritual healing as well. Jesus wanted his listeners to know he can do both. The physical change they saw in the man was evidence of the spiritual change that had also taken place. The religious elite could see Jesus heal the man, but they were unwilling to believe he could forgive sins.

Jesus' question went to the heart of their unbelief. Which is easier—to heal or to forgive?

The question goes to the heart of our unbelief as well. Which is easier: for God to forgive our sins, or to provide the money we need for rent? To forgive our sins, or to give us the precise wisdom we need for our teens? To forgive our sins, or to provide help to fix that broken water heater? To forgive sins, or to strengthen us to face that hard task head on?

Jesus has authority over both.

If you are following Jesus and have trusted him as your Savior, you believe he has the power to forgive your sin. You trusted God with your eternity. Why would we hesitate to trust him for the thirty or fifty or eighty years we spend on earth? So often, the faith that brought us to the cross wears thin when life crashes around us and we find ourselves with problems too big to solve and needs far too great for us to meet.

If we have trusted God for eternal life, we can trust him with every earthly need.

If we have trusted God for eternal life, we can trust him with every earthly need.

What seems unsolvable or insurmountable right now? What is keeping you up at night and causing you to wring your hands in worry? The gospel assures us that God, who sent his Son to walk sinlessly on earth, took our sin upon himself, and defeated death once and for all—this gospel settles conclusively that any problem we're facing this side of heaven is not only under the authority of God, *it is easy for God*.

The Nature of God's Faithfulness

While the gospel assures us we can trust God's faithfulness this side of eternity, our trust can falter because we don't fully understand the nature of God's faithfulness. This was the second thing that helped me cinch God's rock-solid faithfulness—considering the difference between God and ourselves.

We're used to dealing with people who make promises—family, friends, pastors, bosses, peers. As humans, we choose whether to follow through on our promises. I can promise my kids a trip to the beach tomorrow, but if I wake up with a stomach bug or the rain starts up, I can tell you we won't be going.

Some people make promises they never intend to keep. Others have every intention of keeping their promise but reach a point where it's too inconvenient, too costly, or too hard to keep. Promises from people are only as good as their ability and integrity to follow through on them.

Not so with God. God never has to choose to be faithful.[1] He never says, "Today, because I feel especially kind and responsible, I'm going to go ahead and keep that promise for Jessica." Faithfulness is God's very character. It is who he is, and he can be nothing else. That's why God's faithfulness is unchanging.

God's faithfulness is not affected by how impossible your problem seems.

God's faithfulness is not affected by how complicated your situation is.

God's faithfulness is not affected by how unexpected your difficulty is.

God's faithfulness is not affected by the decisions of someone else.

When God says he is faithful, it means that God can only ever be faithful.

When God says he is faithful, it means that God can only ever be faithful.

Billy Graham said, "From one end of the Bible to the other, God assures us that he will never go back on his promises."[2] Look at just a few of the verses about God's unflinching faithfulness.

> Know therefore that the LORD your God is God; he is the faithful God, keeping his covenant of love to a thousand generations of those who love him and keep his commandments.
>
> Deuteronomy 7:9

> Let us hold unswervingly to the hope we profess, for he who promised is faithful.
>
> Hebrews 10:23

> God is not a man, so he does not lie. He is not human, so he does not change his mind. Has he ever spoken and failed to act? Has he ever promised and not carried it through?
>
> Numbers 23:19 NLT

> I saw heaven standing open and there before me was a white horse, whose rider is called Faithful and True.
>
> Revelation 19:11

> Yet this I call to mind and therefore I have hope: Because of the Lord's great love we are not consumed, *for his compassions never fail. They are new every morning; great is your faithfulness.*
>
> Lamentations 3:21–23, emphasis added

Great is God's faithfulness, we often belt out on Sundays. That line is a quote from, of all books, Lamentations, by the prophet Jeremiah after the fall of Jerusalem. Jerusalem was burned, the temple destroyed, leaders and priests deported or killed, and the people taken into slavery.

Through chapters 1, 2, and most of 3, Jeremiah weeps over Jerusalem's ruin until Lamentations 3:21. This verse marks a turn where the prophet declares that despite all the destruction and desolation, he has hope because of God's great love, his unfailing compassion, and his great faithfulness.

The Hebrew word for *love* here is *hesed*. The *h* is pronounced like you're clearing the back of your throat. No single English word is equivalent to *hesed*, but it's often translated as *love, kindness, lovingkindness, mercy, unfailing love, faithful love, steadfast love, and unfailing kindness.* God's *hesed* for us is all of this all at once—a constant and merciful love.

Not only are we held by God's great *hesed*, but Lamentations 3:23 tells us God's compassion never fails. A look at the Hebrew again fleshes out the full meaning of the word *compassion* here—*racham*—which is also used to mean "womb." It's a picture of the constant, protective nurturing and cherishing care a mother has for her child in her womb.

Lamentations 3:23 then tells us God's great faithfulness is new every morning, as certain as the sun rising every day. When was the last time you wrung your hands over whether the sun would come up the next day? I'd venture to guess you've never done it. We don't even give it a second thought. We set our alarm clocks, make plans for the next day, and go to sleep in bold confidence that the sun will come up just as it always has.

That is God's faithfulness. It is as absolute as the sunrise.

God's faithfulness is inexhaustible. You will never reach a quota where God's faithfulness has been used up. God's compassion isn't new in the sense that he has to renew it every morning, but it's fresh in the sense that no matter what new circumstances we find ourselves in, we find God faithful there too.

God's faithfulness is uninterrupted. It's more than the promise that God *will be* faithful; it's that God is *right now* being faithful. His faithfulness doesn't start and stop. You may not see it currently, but you can be certain (as the sun coming up tomorrow) that God's faithfulness is at work!

There's one more thing we can do when we question whether God will be faithful: We can look back to all the times he's been faithful to us in the past.

When I'm facing a new scary step of faith, I often say to myself, *Lisa, God did not get you this far to drop you now.*

We need to stop and intentionally recall the times in the past when we faced the hard or impossible and God guided us through. Think of a time when you didn't have enough money and God provided. Remember a situation when you didn't have the skill or ability needed and God equipped you. Remember a season of waiting when God's timing was better than you could have asked or imagined.

If you are questioning, *Will God be faithful in this, to me?* remember God can only be faithful. It's as constant and certain as tomorrow's sunrise. And he has not taken you this far to drop you now. In fact, God is acting in perfect faithfulness for you right this second.

What Has God Promised?

Okay then, you might be thinking, *Why didn't God give me the answer I prayed for? Why am I still waiting for help? Why didn't he do what I asked?*

To be sure, God could do it, whatever *it* is. Nothing is impossible with God. He holds all power and he controls all power. But the power of God is always tempered by the will of God.

When Jesus prayed in the garden of Gethsemane before his crucifixion, he asked God to keep him from suffering and death. He knew God could do it, but he also knew God exercised his power according to his will. "'Abba, Father,' he said, 'everything is possible for you. Take this cup from me. Yet not what I will, but what you will'" (Mark 14:36).

I had begged God to heal Dan. I prayed for days after Dan's death for God to resuscitate him—I mean, he did it for Lazarus, couldn't he do it for us? Yes. Yes, he could. But, like Jesus in the garden, the power of God is tempered by the will of God. God does not always take the cup of suffering from us.

I had also prayed another prayer. Pacing my living room floor, as paramedics worked on Dan in our bedroom, I had begged God for mercy. This is a prayer God has answered over and over since Dan died. As I write this a few years out from that traumatic morning, I can see all the big and little ways God has answered that prayer. Not the way I wanted—by sparing Dan's life—but the way he willed to rescue me again and again and again through grueling heartache.

God's will is reflected in his promises.

Depending on how they're counted, the Bible has more than 7,700 promises.[3] If we put one promise each day on a flip calendar, it would take more than twenty-one years to cover all the promises. Some of them are specific promises God made to one person or one nation. When God told Joshua, "I will give you every place where you set your foot, as I promised Moses,"[4] it was a promise specific to Joshua as the Israelites were entering the Promised Land. I can't walk around a dream house and claim God has promised it to me.

Even so, the Bible has many, many promises that apply broadly to all those who follow him. These promises never change, even when our circumstances change. Those changed circumstances, though, reveal holes in the solid foundation we thought we had. We may think we've built our life on God's promises, but when loss strips away people or jobs or a certain future, we realize how much those things were holding us up. We need to re-anchor in the promises.

I had to do this after Dan died. We had been a single-income family, and Dan's was the sole income. Years before, I had practiced law and loved it, but as I had children, I went from full-time to part-time to flex time. Then after the birth of my fourth child, we took a huge leap to give up any second income and supported our growing family through Dan's job alone. As the years passed, I decided to formally retire from law, which meant if I ever went back, I'd have to take the bar exam again. But what were the chances I'd need to go back?

Then, suddenly, I was a single mom of seven and, though we had some safety net, I was scared to pieces over my finances and how to support my family long-term.

But my fear was based on a lie. God didn't promise that I'd always have a husband who would always have a job. God promised to meet all our needs according to his riches in Christ Jesus.[5] For a while, God met our needs as both Dan and I worked, and then for many years, God met our needs through Dan's job alone. And in this new season, God continued to meet our needs. His promise held, even though everything looked different. God simply provided through different means.

Sometimes God met our needs through the generosity of family and friends who reached out to help. Sometimes he provided through the work I was able to do from home around my children's schedules. Later, he opened opportunities for me to write and speak. I've watched God meet my children's financial needs through college scholarships, jobs, housing opportunities, and friends who gave them cars they no longer needed.

Your changed circumstance will never alter the unchangeable promises of God.

Your changed circumstance will never alter the unchangeable promises of God.

Nothing can amend the promises of God. No person, no job, no unexpected death or divorce or diagnosis. Though the devil works to get us to doubt God's promise, that is the sole extent of his ability. The enemy cannot keep God from fulfilling his promise; he can only keep us doubting along the way. Rest assured that if God has promised it, neither the enemy nor anything else in all creation can prevent him from fulfilling it.

In your changed circumstances, find God's promises that speak to your current need and lean on them. Let's look at a few of God's 7,700 promises you can count on.

God promises comfort in any situation. "Praise be to the God and Father of our Lord Jesus Christ, the Father of compassion and the God of all comfort, who comforts us in all our troubles, so that we can comfort those in any trouble with the comfort we ourselves receive from God" (2 Corinthians 1:3–4).

God promises to give you wisdom. "And if, in the process, any of you does not know how to meet any particular problem he has only to ask God—who gives generously to all men without making them feel foolish or guilty—and he may be quite sure that the necessary wisdom will be given him" (James 1:5 Phillips).

God promises to meet your needs. "And God is able to make all grace abound to you, so that having all sufficiency in all things at all times, you may abound in every good work" (2 Corinthians 9:8 ESV).

God promises to guide you. "Trust in the LORD with all your heart; do not depend on your own understanding. Seek his will in all you do, and he will show you which path to take" (Proverbs 3:5–6 NLT).

God promises to give you strength. "He gives strength to the weary and increases the power of the weak. Even youths grow tired and weary, and young men stumble and fall; but those who hope in the LORD will renew their strength" (Isaiah 40:29–31).

God promises to be present with you. "The Lord is close to the brokenhearted and saves those who are crushed in spirit." (Psalm 34:18).

God promises he will never forsake you. "God has said, 'Never will I leave you; never will I forsake you'" (Hebrews 13:5).

God promises rest in weariness. "Come to me, all who labor and are heavy laden, and I will give you rest" (Matthew 11:28 ESV).

God promises he will bring a harvest from your work. "Let us not become weary in doing good, for at the proper time we will reap a harvest if we do not give up" (Galatians 6:9).

At the end of this book, I've listed forty promises from God that you can count on as you find your footing. Read through the promises and underline or highlight those that you need now.

A Prayer to Deepen Faith

Lord, I don't want to be a fair-weather believer. But only you can strengthen my faith when questions rise to the top. Tether me to you and help me trust you no matter what. You have always been faithful to me. Your record is 100 percent. You have not taken me this far to drop me now. You are my firm foundation and my sure hope even when I cannot yet see. Reveal my unbelief and chisel every bit out so you have my undivided heart. In Jesus' name, amen.

5

The God Who Is for You

> See, I have engraved you on the palms of my hands; your walls are ever before me.
>
> Isaiah 49:16

> Faith is deliberate confidence in the character of God whose ways you may not understand at the time.
>
> Oswald Chambers

In the last chapter, we answered the question of whether God will be faithful to us, in our particular circumstance, with an all-caps YES. We found that we can count on his faithfulness as we count on the sun coming up tomorrow. It's not *whether* God will keep his promises, but *when* he will fulfill them and how it will look. Even knowing this, though, you may find yourself battling to prop up your faith.

Our faith wilts not because our problems are too big but because our view of God is too small.

The more we understand who God is, the easier it is to trust him. In my own experience, this was life-changing insight I needed to help me trust when I could not see.

My prayer is that you will never see God the same again after reading this chapter. And that with your understanding of God aligned to who he says he is, you will never doubt God again either. When we begin to understand God's infinite greatness, we realize it's crazy *not* to trust him.

We won't know God in his fullness until we see him face-to-face in heaven, but until then, we can ask God to help us spiritually discern as much as humanly possible about his character.[1] Pull out a highlighter and get your pen ready, and let's ask God to help us wrap as much of our finite minds as possible around the breathtaking, jaw-dropping wonder of who he is.

1. God is great.

> "No one is like you, Lord; you are great, and your name is mighty in power" (Jeremiah 10:6).

> "There is no one holy like the Lord; there is no one besides you; there is no Rock like our God" (1 Samuel 2:2).

The word *great* has become so common and overused that it's now a flavorless catch-all word. How are you doing? Great. How was the movie? Great. Let's meet for lunch at noon. Great. The word no longer holds the nuance or context it once did.

So the first thing we have to do to understand what the Bible means when it says "God is great" is to set aside our bland version of the word.

The second problem comes because we often say, "God is greater." He's greater than our sin. He's greater than the enemy.

He's greater than our circumstances. And all of that is true—God is greater than anything or anyone in the seen or unseen world. However, when we say God is greater, it brings to mind a yardstick. At the lower end is humanity in all our frailty, or perhaps Satan with his limited authority, or our circumstances that bow to the sovereignty of God. We imagine God, who is greater, at the other end of this yardstick.

The error comes because, in reality, God is not even on the yardstick. It's not that God is great*er*. It's that God is *great*. Measureless. He exists outside of any limit or scale whatsoever, whether it's a measure of power, time, knowledge, or anything else.

God alone is uncreated and infinite. Everything else is created and finite, including us. And when we try to stretch our mind and imagination to fully take in the greatness of God, we have already limited him. God is great beyond anything we will ever be able to wrap our minds around this side of heaven.

God's greatness is not simply an adjective describing who he is. It is a verb describing what he does. God is great and God does great things. He is great to us in ways that are beyond comparison. That's why Isaiah 55:8–9 tells us, "'For my thoughts are not your thoughts, neither are your ways my ways,' declares the LORD. 'As the heavens are higher than the earth, so are my ways higher than your ways and my thoughts than your thoughts.'"

God's greatness is not simply an adjective describing who he is. It is a verb describing what he does.

When we begin to wring our hands at our circumstances or despair that there's no way for God to bring us through, let's instead camp in the truth that God is jaw-droppingly, unfathomably great, and he is great to us.

> Great is the LORD and most worthy of praise; his greatness no one can fathom.
>
> Psalm 145:3

> He does great and unsearchable things, wonders without number.
>
> Job 9:10 CSB

2. God is all-powerful.

This isn't news to us. Most of us would easily agree that God is not just powerful, but has all power. God can do anything. The problem is that while we acknowledge God is all-powerful with our words, we don't always embrace it with our heart.

When life is going along in a fairly normal rhythm, we say with the best of them that God can do anything. But then we come face first with a mountain too steep to climb and too formidable to see our way around. That's when the gap between what we say and what we believe is revealed. We often pray something like this: "God, here is my big need. But it's big. And super hard. Actually, it looks impossible." And just like that, we shrink God down to the size of our difficulty.

Nothing is hard or easy for God. Those are conditions that describe limited ability and limited resources. If God is infinitely powerful, there is no hard or easy for him. There is only done or not done.[2]

Understanding this has changed the way I pray. For years, I kind of held my breath when asking God to do something big. "Pray big," a friend often reminded me, but I worried it was too big and too hard. But I see now there are no scales with God. Over the last few years, I've prayed very precise prayers. I used to think this was too picky. What were the chances he'd answer it? But I now see it's so picky that only God could bring it about. And if he chooses to do so, I'll 100 percent know that it was all and only God.

Not only does God have all power, he also controls all power. God is sovereign over every boss, every government official, every twenty-four-hour day. God is in control over nature and over the enemy.

The best way for us to begin comprehending that God is all-powerful is to see how often God declares it in his Word.

When Abraham was ninety-nine years old and his wife, Sarah, was eighty-nine, God told them they would have a son within the year. Sarah laughed (it's hard to blame her!), but God responded: "Is anything too hard for the LORD? I will return to you at the appointed time next year, and Sarah will have a son" (Genesis 18:14). And out of physically impossible circumstances, God fulfilled his promise.

> For nothing will be impossible with God.
>
> Luke 1:37 ESV

> Jesus looked at them and said, "With man this is impossible, but not with God; all things are possible with God."
>
> Mark 10:27

> Jesus prayed: "Abba, Father," he said, "everything is possible for you. Take this cup from me."
>
> Mark 14:36

> This is what the LORD of Heaven's Armies says: All this may seem impossible to you now, a small remnant of God's people. But is it impossible for me? says the LORD of Heaven's Armies.
>
> Zechariah 8:6 NLT

> Ah Sovereign LORD, you have made the heavens and the earth by your great power and outstretched arm. Nothing is too hard for you.
>
> Jeremiah 32:17

> I am the LORD, the God of all mankind. Is anything too hard for me?
>
> Jeremiah 32:27

> I know that you can do anything, and no can stop you.
>
> Job 42:2 NLT

Maybe you have marked off a problem in your life as too hard for God. Maybe you've prayed about it while telling yourself it's too hard to believe God would hear you. How does it change your prayers to know that nothing you encounter is impossible for God? Know this:

> No need is too great for God to provide.
> No sadness is too heavy for God to comfort.
> No circumstance is too ugly for God to redeem.
> No temptation is too strong for God to deliver.
> No relationship is too broken for God to repair.
> No sin is too horrible for God to pardon.
> No sin cycle is too strong for God to break.
> No wound is too deep for God to heal.
> No person is too far for God to save.
> *Nothing is impossible with God.*

3. God is all-knowing.

Do you ever feel like God isn't paying attention to what's going on in your life? Like he is taking care of everyone else but is overlooking you?

God knows you better than you could ever know yourself. The Psalms say, "O Lord, you have examined my heart and know everything about me. You know when I sit down or stand up. You know my thoughts even when I'm far away. . . . You know everything I do. You know what I am going to say even before I say it, Lord. . . . Such knowledge is too wonderful for me, too great for me to understand!" (Psalm 139:1–4, 6 NLT). God knows everything about you, your children, your relationships, your work, your dreams, your pain, and your deepest desires. God knows every tiny detail of every circumstance in your life. Nothing is hidden from him, and there's nothing he needs to discover.

God knows the intricacies of every cell in your body, the thousands of thoughts racing through your mind, the motives driving your actions and reactions, the emotions that bubble up, and those too deep to name. God knows every moment of your past and all the moments yet to be.

God knows your needs before you ever pray them. He asks us to pray, not because he needs an update, but because we need to go to him, fix our eyes on him, and depend on him.

God knows the worries and what-ifs that keep you sleepless at night. He knows the weight of everything you carry—the regret, hurt, despair, loneliness, anger, remorse, and wishing things were different. God knows the things we're too ashamed to even admit to ourselves, much less anyone else. He's always known them.

Even when we can't see God's hand, God is always at work. "The steadfast love of the Lord never ceases" (Lamentations 3:22 ESV).

God knows you fully and completely—and God loves you wildly. He always has.

God is not only all-knowing, but he is all-wise. He knows your struggles and the solutions. He knows the way he's taking you and how to get you there. He knows your needs and how he will meet them.

I saw this so personally about a year after Dan died. I walked out to the garage to find my then six-year-old shooting a BB gun in the backyard. He'd gotten it out of the locked cabinet in the tool chest. I was horrified. I had a firm conversation with him about gun safety, about needing adult permission and supervision, and locked the gun back up. He nodded with a sober "yes, ma'am," but a few days later, I walked into the garage and saw him shooting the BB gun again! This time, I didn't hold back. I took the gun, lectured solidly, and told him it would be gone if he ever did it again. He teared up with an apology, and I went inside to the laundry room, shut the door, and buried my head in a pile of towels and sobbed. I knew in my gut the problem wasn't disobedience. The problem was he needed a dad. The BB gun was a connection with his father. As hard as I tried to be a good mom, I couldn't be his dad.

Within the hour, my cell phone buzzed. It was a friend telling me her husband wanted to have my six-year-old and another of his brothers to their farm. Was there anything special they could do with them? Oh. Yes. Her husband was a bird hunter, so I asked if he'd take my little boy out, let him shoot on their property to his heart's content, and talk to him about handling guns. While I had sobbed a prayer of tears on those towels, God was orchestrating his answer. He had the answer before I even had the need.

Does realizing that God knows your need and the solution better than you help you trust him? Does it help you release control and trust God with your children, your finances, or your tangled circumstance?

4. God is all-present.

While God is powerfully sovereign over the universe, he is also tenderly present in us.

God says he is close to the brokenhearted,[3] and that's almost an understatement. In the early weeks and months after Dan's death, God's presence cloaked me in a way I've never known. It was palpable. I felt as though God was both holding me up and giving me a soft landing. I was in constant prayer—a running dialogue of asking questions, seeking guidance, unburdening my heart, and begging for help.

While God is powerfully sovereign over the universe, he is also tenderly present in us.

It's important to note that God's presence didn't deaden the pain. The pain was still very real—a raw, physical ache like my insides had been hollowed out. It didn't take away the sting of loneliness or the gaping hole I felt at every dinner, in every conversation, and with every decision.

And yet, there in my darkest season, God had never felt nearer.

Maybe you don't palpably feel God's presence, and he feels further away than ever right now. You're not alone in wondering where God is. Even Bible superstars like David, a man after God's own heart, wrestled with feeling God was distant.

In Psalm 22, David cried out, "God, my God! Why would you abandon me now? Why do you remain distant, refusing to answer my tearful cries in the day and my desperate cries for your help in the night? . . . *Where are you, my God?*" (Psalm 22:1–2 TPT, emphasis added).

When God feels far away, it helps to saturate our mind with truth until our feelings catch up. This is what David did. While he didn't hold back his questions and feelings, David also preached truth to himself. Look at the next verses in Psalm 22: "Yet I know that you are most holy. You are God-Enthroned, the praise of Israel. Our fathers' faith was in you—through the generations they trusted in you *and you came through*" (vv. 3–4 TPT, emphasis added). You can be sure God will come through for you too. Though God may feel distant, he has not moved.

You cannot go anywhere that God is not. You may not feel God present with you or sense him guiding you, but our feelings are not the test of what is true. We are anchored in God not because we feel it, but because God holds us in the worst storms and highest waves.

For most of my life, I thought that part of God was with me, part with you, and part with the people across the world. But God's presence cannot be divided like so many little packages. Rather, the complete, infinite fullness of God dwells with me, and the complete, infinite fullness of God dwells with you. We each abide in the full, indivisible presence of God. Whether our feelings confirm it or not, *you have all of God all the time.*

God created time itself, which means he is not bound by time as we are. God is in our past, present, and future all at once. We wait for outcomes; God is already there. Time limits us so that we experience life sequentially. Not so with God. God is not waiting to see what will happen in the future, because he is already there as much as he is here in the present.

How does knowing that the fullness of God's presence is here with you now—with all his wisdom, goodness, kindness, peace, and love—bring you comfort? Does realizing God knows your tomorrows and is already there give peace to your concerns about the future?

5. God is infinitely sufficient.

When I hear the word *sufficient*, I think "just enough." If I have sufficient gas for a trip, I have just enough to get there without getting stranded on the interstate. Or if I have sufficient food in the pantry, we'll make it through the week, but we'll run out eventually and I'll need to restock.

God's sufficiency is not just enough but more than enough. God's resources are measureless. They never run out. He has never known need, never known want, never had to cast about for how he will provide for us.

God's infinite sufficiency means that he has every resource imaginable to meet our needs. Philippians 4:19 says, "And my God will meet all your needs according to his glorious riches in Christ Jesus." But God's sufficiency goes beyond material needs.

Second Corinthians 9:8 tells us God is more than enough to meet any need in any circumstances: "And God is able to bless you abundantly, so that in all things at all times, having all that you need, you will abound in every good work." When we get to a place where we feel incapable, too weak for our circumstances, or too weary to continue, God's grace is more than enough: "My grace is sufficient for you, for my power is made perfect in weakness" (2 Corinthians 12:9).

God is infinitely sufficient whether we believe it or not. He is infinitely sufficient regardless of whether we feel it or not. And he is infinitely sufficient whether we take him up on it or not.

When you don't feel up to the task ahead of you, how does knowing God has every resource you need help you to move forward? How does God's infinite sufficiency help you trust him in your current circumstance?

6. God is unchanging.

We live in a world of constant change. Things grow and decay. We have new diseases and new cures. Economies surge and stall. Ocean levels rise and weather patterns shift. The very plates on which we are walking are moving, creating earthquakes, tsunamis, erosion, and volcanic explosions. Our jobs, our friends, and our relationships change. Yet we can be certain that no matter what changes rock our world, God our Rock never changes.

God is immutable. That sounds heady and theological, but it is a true comfort when we're navigating the unexpected. Here's what I mean:

Our circumstances may change, but our circumstances never change God. He is always good, always kind, always just, always merciful, always sovereign. "For the LORD is good. His unfailing love continues forever, and his faithfulness continues to each generation" (Psalm 100:5 NLT).

God's will for each of us personally and for the world never changes. "But the LORD's plans stand firm forever; his intentions can never be shaken" (Psalm 33:11 NLT).

God's promises never change. They will never be rescinded, modified, added to, or changed in any way. "I make known the end from the beginning, from ancient times, what is still to come. I say, 'My purpose will stand, and I will do all that I please'" (Isaiah 46:10).

God and his Word are unchangeable and are the only anchors when life shifts. If we expect the economy, a person, a relationship, a job, our health, a church, or anything other than God to anchor us, we will be disappointed every time.

What are some things you've tried to anchor your life with? How does knowing that God and his promises are unchangeable help you navigate this unexpected season?

7. God loves you infinitely.

It's easy to believe God loves us when we're living the life we ordered. But when the tables are flipped and life doles out pain and difficulty instead, the first thing we often doubt is God's love for us.

Why would a loving God allow this? we wonder. *Why wouldn't a loving God get me out of this?* But the measure of God's love is never our circumstances; the measure of God's love is the cross.[4]

God so loved the world that he gave his one and only Son to pay the cost of our sin, and to restore our relationship with him both here and eternally. We know what it is to love as a human—as a mother or spouse or child. But we could not fully understand God's divine, unconditional, perfect, complete, infinite love for us if we tried.

We can, though, refuse the doubts that muddy our acceptance of God's great love.

We can choose to believe God loves us and is acting in perfect love for us even if our prayer wasn't answered the way we hoped, if the wait is longer than we expected, or if we're walking a path we never wanted.

Keeping our minds centered on God's infinite love secures us. Although we won't be able to fully comprehend God's love until we get to heaven, we can use this prayer from Ephesians to ask God to help us understand:

> And I pray that you, being rooted and established in love, may have power, together with all the Lord's holy people, to grasp how wide and long and high and deep is the love of Christ, and to know this love that surpasses knowledge—that you may be filled to the measure of all the fullness of God.
>
> Ephesians 3:17–19

If you could fully accept God's infinite love for you, how would that change your trust, your perception of your current struggle, your response, and your ability to wait on God?

This is the God who is for you. The God who is incomparably great, unfathomably powerful, infinitely knowing and wise, fully present, wholly sufficient, forever constant, and extravagantly loving to you, with you, *and for you.*

And we've only considered the fringe of his splendor.[5] When you're walking through a painful season, you need to know in the depths of your bones that this is the God who is for you.

He is the God who fights for you, who goes before you, who has written your name on the palm of his hand,[6] who intercedes for you, and who will bring you through. We would be crazy not to trust him.

A Prayer to God Who Is for You

Dear God, I have allowed doubt to steal my security in you because I couldn't comprehend how great you are. Forgive me for making you a god in my own image and help me to worship you as God Almighty. Thank you for your presence, all-sufficiency, and incredible love, and that you are the same yesterday, today, and forever. Not one need in my life is impossible for you. You are worthy of all praise and all honor and all my trust. In Jesus' name, amen.

6

Make Space for Deep Grace

"My grace is always more than enough for you, and my power finds its full expression through your weakness."

2 Corinthians 12:9 TPT

Beloved Christian reader, in matters of grace you need a daily supply. . . . Never go hungry while the daily bread of grace is on the table of mercy.

C. H. Spurgeon

"I'll never forget when I got the phone call telling me that something was wrong with Avery." Sarah, a fellow writer and mom of three, had a normal pregnancy and delivery with Avery, her youngest, but when Avery was three months old, Sarah witnessed her baby's first forty-minute seizure. "I couldn't imagine that something was actually wrong with my perfectly healthy three-month-old."

For the next year, Avery continued to have numerous seizures followed by emergency room visits, hospital stays, and tests while doctors worked to come up with a diagnosis. Eventually, a diagnosis came: Dravet syndrome—a lifelong, catastrophic form of epilepsy.

"I remember the darkness really overtaking me and recognizing that nothing would ever be the same again," said Sarah. "Her future wouldn't be the same, our family wouldn't be the same, life as we knew it would be different." Sarah later told me that one of the hardest points for her was realizing God might not take Avery's condition away. She grew angry and upset, and says she "got real with God." Eventually, she knew she had a choice: walk away from God completely or choose to trust him even when she didn't understand the situation. She chose to trust God no matter what.

"When everything is going well, it's easy to rely on yourself, whereas when every day feels weighty and heavy and overwhelming, it's just full reliance on his grace to make it through," Sarah says. "I wake up in the morning, saying, 'God, I can't do this. I need you to help me, because in my humanity, I can't do this.'"

Sarah credits God's "steady presence" as the grace that sustained her through her worst days. "The biggest thing I've taken away from this journey is that God is faithful, and even in those dark places, even on the hardest days, he never left us and he never will."

God's Grace Sustains

Before Dan died, if you would have asked me about God's grace, I would have told you about salvation—God's unmerited favor, which covered the cost for our sin and gives us eternal life when we repent and follow Christ.

But God's grace doesn't stop there. God's grace is more than a one-time offer. It's there for us after we're saved, carrying us through every staggering circumstance, every painful difficulty, and every stretching struggle we go through this side of heaven. We would be hopeless without God's saving grace, and also without his sustaining grace.

It's this sustaining grace we come to know so well when we're neck-deep in difficulty. Becoming a believer doesn't mean we get a free pass from trouble. We're all part of a fallen world, a world scarred and impacted by sin. God hasn't taken Christians out of the world; he hasn't immunized us from the effects of sin, like disease and economic collapse, infidelity and death.

God will either move the mountain in front of us or give us his grace for the climb.

God will either move the mountain in front of us or give us his grace for the climb.

Paul describes his experience of God's sustaining grace in 2 Corinthians 12:7–10 (emphasis added):

> Therefore, in order to keep me from becoming conceited, I was given a thorn in my flesh, a messenger of Satan, to torment me. Three times I pleaded with the Lord to take it away from me. But he said to me, "**My grace is sufficient for you, for my power is made perfect in weakness.**" Therefore I will boast all the more gladly about my weaknesses, so that Christ's power may rest on me. That is why, for Christ's sake, I delight in weaknesses, in insults, in hardships, in persecutions, in difficulties. **For when I am weak, then I am strong.**

Hold on, here. Paul chose to delight in the very things I beg God to keep me from? That seems a high bar, maybe one for ultra-Christian elites like Paul. But delight isn't reserved for a select few. It's for ordinary believers like you and me because it's in our suffering and difficulty that God transforms our ordinary lives to an extraordinary witness through his sustaining grace.

Paul didn't trudge through suffering as if he'd gotten the leftovers of life; he thought about suffering as good because it was there his weakness became a catalyst for God's power.

Now, to be fair, Paul begged God to take the thorn away on three occasions. Scripture gives no details about the nature of the thorn. We're not told whether it was another person tormenting Paul, a chronic health condition, or an emotional or psychological issue. Because Scripture never names the particular thorn, we can apply it broadly to the deep difficulties we face.

Despite Paul's pleas, God didn't remove the thorn. Instead, God gave him sustaining grace to endure.

When God doesn't rescue us from suffering, we can be quick to accuse him.

Have you ever begged God day after day to either take something from you or do something for you, yet you didn't see it happen? The first thing we usually do when we've got a tormenting thorn is ask God to make it stop, take it away, or bring it to an end. And when God doesn't do this, we often think God hasn't answered. The conversation turns from *God, please do this*, to *God, are you even listening? Are you paying attention? Because I'm praying and nothing is happening.*

Each time Paul prayed, God listened. He wasn't ignoring Paul, turning his back on him, or getting too distracted with other matters to deal with this. We know God heard Paul's prayer because God's answer is recorded for us.

God's answer may be the same for you—*My grace is sufficient for you.*

God loves you too much to ignore you; he would never turn his back on you and he can't be distracted from you. His eye is always on you, and he knows your pain and the longings of your heart. Sometimes, in his perfect love, God fixes the circumstance causing us pain. But other times, in that same perfect love, God gives us a path we would never choose. In those times, God's perfect love means leaving the thorn but giving us his sustaining grace.

Another accusation we often make against God is unfairness. You're in good company if you've ever told God you don't deserve something. Or if you've questioned why those who couldn't care less about God are living their best life while yours is in shards around you.

Maybe, like me, you've filed a grievance with God along with a list of all you've done for him. After Dan died, I didn't petulantly stomp my foot against God. My accusation was disguised with a reminder of our "deal." We'd gone out on a limb to trust God with however many children he wanted to give us, and when I had a child in my late thirties and another in my early forties, I assumed God would let Dan live to see them grown and flown. *Why would you call us to step out in faith and then allow this? Don't you know what we've given up and how foolish our trust looks now?*

Paul more than any of us could have presented his list of good deeds to God. He'd had a promising position as a Pharisee, where he was quickly rising through the ranks. But he gave it all up to follow Jesus. While planting churches and preaching the gospel across Asia and Europe, Paul endured beatings, whippings, stoning, shipwrecks, prison, slander, rejection, weariness, hunger, thirst, cold, false teachers, and false doctrine. Yet not once did Paul resent God for not taking the thorn from him. In fact, though he begged God to take it, Paul came to realize that God's sustaining grace was better. Paul's weakness allowed God's power to be fully at work through him.

Most of us want to see God's power in our life, but none of us want to be weak enough to depend on it. But in God's kingdom, that's how it works. That difficulty God hasn't removed in your life is the very difficulty where God's power shows up in us. When we're too weary to push through, God's power is made perfect. In our inability to do that task, God's power is made perfect. It's moment-by-moment grace that carries us through the deepest pain.

God's grace is stamina when we're too weary to keep going.

God's grace is comfort when the pain is more than we can bear.

God's grace is endurance when we're waiting longer than we dreamed possible.

God's grace is courage when the step ahead is too hard.

It's only when we reach a point of utter weakness that we see God's supernatural strength.

If we will surrender to God instead of accusing God, we will come to see God's sustaining grace as the better way.

Most of us want to see God's power in our life, but none of us want to be weak enough to depend on it.

God never made the kind of deal I thought I'd signed up for. His call to trust him with our children was a call to trust *him*; it wasn't *my* plan or how I wanted it to look. I've had a front row seat to God's power in pain and weakness. God has fathered my children through family members, Sunday school teachers, coaches, youth pastors and leaders, and other men who have stepped in over and over again. It doesn't mean my kids and I don't dearly miss Dan. God did not take this thorn from us, but he most certainly gave us his grace and provision to walk through it.

When Paul wrote about the thorn in his flesh in 2 Corinthians, he'd endured it for fourteen years. From his own experience, Paul could look back over those fourteen years and see that God's grace and power that came through his weakness far surpassed his original desire for God to remove it. I wonder how often God's reassurance that his grace was enough held Paul through other hard circumstances. I wonder if God's words echoed when Paul was imprisoned, when friends and followers abandoned him, when he was weary and on the run. Tradition tells us that after languishing in a Roman prison, Paul was martyred by the brutally wicked emperor Nero. I wonder if, just before Paul took his last breaths, God's words bathed him with supernatural peace: *My grace is sufficient for you.*

Give Yourself Grace

We not only need God's grace to get through difficulty, but we also need to give ourselves grace. Though God lavishes us with grace, we can be much harder on ourselves than God is. We set ourselves up with expectations and timelines we would never impose on someone else. And when we aren't able to do what we think we should, the critical self-talk kicks into high gear.

This season of difficulty you are in now differs from other seasons, and what you are able to do in this season is different as well. Your life has changed, and it may never look the same again. When life falls apart, it affects family, friendships, work, passions, interests, finances, and our daily energy and sleep.

Give yourself the beautiful gift of grace. You need large pockets of time and space to process big and hard emotions. Emotions don't come when it's convenient or when we have ample energy and resources. They come in deep waves that demand all our focus and attention and then some, which necessarily affects other commitments. This is the season to know when to say no to other demands, to give yourself plenty of margin for slow days of needed rest, for counseling, for journaling and processing, and for the extra tasks that come with life change.

Give yourself grace if you can't keep your house up to the standards you want, if you don't have a home-cooked dinner on the table every night, or if you've had to let the yard go a bit. There were many nights in the months after Dan died when we had cereal for dinner or ate leftovers in front of the television.

Because you know what's more important than dusty baseboards and cereal for dinner? You. You and your heart and the people in your home need tremendous attention and energy right now, and it is right and good to let other things go in this season.

The grace you give yourself is more beautiful than a picture-perfect home could ever be.

Extending grace to yourself also means letting go of guilt and regret. It's easy to look back and wish we had done something different. Boy, can we beat ourselves up by replaying memories of what was and then punishing ourselves for what we didn't do—or did do.

I regretted not making Dan's health more of a priority. I regretted not getting CPR certified. *You gave so much attention to raising your kids and you neglected your husband,* I chided myself. Guilt and regret are always part of deep disappointment, but we have to give ourselves the same grace God gives us. We did the best we knew, and we need to let God's grace cover where we fell short.

And give yourself the grace of self-care. Jesus commanded us to love our neighbors as we love ourselves. When our own soul, mind, and body are well nurtured, we can love others well. Self-care might mean giving yourself a day off to tuck in at home or an afternoon to window shop and think your own thoughts. It might mean getting outside to walk or run or meet up with a friend for coffee. It might mean saying no to yardwork and saying yes to a family day of doing something fun together. Counter the toll that emotions and big changes take by giving yourself grace to refuel and refill.

Grace for Everyone Else

There's one more area where we will need lots of grace as we navigate this unexpected and unwanted season: We'll need to extend grace to those around us.

First, for the people in our homes. Everyone deals with deep emotions and change differently, and that goes for the people in your home. My teen boys wanted everything to go back to normal as quickly as possible. I was surprised they asked to go to church two days after their dad had passed away, when I couldn't bear the questions or conversations that would come. We compromised, sneaking into the top row of the balcony after the service started and leaving before it dismissed.

Give your family lots of grace for longer than you think you will need it. So long as it's healthy, allow each person to process their hard emotions on their timetable and in the way that feels right for them.

You'll also need grace for your extended family, neighbors, friends, and colleagues. Someone will say something that lands hard or hurtfully for you, though they mean for it to help. Give them grace.

Some people in your circle may not say anything at all because they're paralyzed with not knowing what to say. Give them grace.

Some people will tell you to call them, and you know as they say it, you never will, because it was a token offer meant to show they're sorry for your circumstance. Give them grace.

If friendships change, colleagues walk on eggshells around you for months, or pastors or staff members at your church don't respond the way you wish they would, give them grace. I think most people are well-meaning, and many just don't know how to respond.

If we don't extend grace, these wrongs become festering new wounds that keep us from moving forward well. You have too much to carry right now without piling on new grievances and irritations.

This is a season for deep, continual, rich grace. I pray you come face-to-face with deep grace like never before. Cling to God's sustaining grace when pain, loneliness, or weariness threatens to undo you. Let grace saturate your heart and the expectations you place on yourself. And let grace reign in your home and in your relationships.

Remember Sarah and her youngest, Avery, who you met at the beginning of this chapter? Life hasn't been easy, but it's been good. Sarah says, "We've seen so many miracles along the way. In every smile, in every word spoken, in every new experience that she gets to have . . . the biggest thing I've taken away from this journey is that God is faithful and, even in those dark places, even on the hardest days, he never left us and he never will. And for that I'm so grateful. For the life of Avery and each day we get to have with her, we're so grateful. She's pretty amazing."

May grace leave a far deeper mark on your life than your circumstances.

When life changed suddenly for my family, I sat down and wrote a Grace Guide for Hard Seasons. I needed a tangible reminder to give myself abundant grace and to extend it to my children and others as life looked different. You can find a copy of this guide in appendix B.

A Prayer for Grace-Filled Living

Heavenly Father, your grace has saved me, and your grace will sustain me. I am not enough, but you are more than enough. In my weakness, give me your strength to do hard things. In my weariness, give me your stamina to take care of the tasks you've called me to. In my woundedness, help me extend your grace to those around me. Thank you for waking me to your renewed mercy this morning. In Jesus' name, amen.

7

Desperate for Good in a Life Gone Bad

Do not be anxious about anything, but in every situation, by prayer and petition, with thanksgiving, present your requests to God. And the peace of God, which transcends all understanding, will guard your hearts and minds in Christ Jesus.

Philippians 4:6–7

The key to thankfulness is not to view God through the lens of our circumstances, but to view our circumstances through the lens of God's love and sovereign purpose.

Anne Graham Lotz

The day Dan died, June 17, became the divider of my life into two parts. Before that date was the good life I wanted. It wasn't perfect by any means, but it was the life

I'd planned, the life I'd chosen and worked for, the life brimming with a bucket list of dreams, happiness, and goodness.

After June 17, everything felt permanently shifted, and all I wanted, worked toward, and eagerly anticipated was buried with Dan. Though I showed up to cheer my kids on at games, went back to activities at church, and made small-talk at gatherings with friends, inside I was a shell of my former self. When the grocery clerk smiled at checkout and asked if I'd found everything I wanted, I'd politely say yes while my insides howled, "If you only knew! I left my heart in aisle 11 with the Pellegrino I no longer put into my cart for my husband!"

Every moment was laced with a screaming reminder of what life should have looked like. Every new challenge was a blaring siren of all that I was carrying alone. While I'd always heard time heals all wounds, time worked against me as the initial fog of loss wore off and a brutal reality set in.

One night, when the kids were in bed and my hands were wrist-deep in sudsy dishwater, I thought, *I hate my life. This isn't the life I ordered. I had the life I wanted and now I'm stuck here.*

This wasn't a "season." This was the rest of my life, and all I could see was endless pain and layers of loss.

In a life that felt excruciatingly bad, I desperately needed to see good. I mean, I agreed with Scripture and the Sunday morning songs that declared God is good, but I needed to *see* that goodness here, for me, and now. I needed evidence that life this side of that June 17 fulcrum might not be what I'd chosen, but it could still be good.

I wish I could tell you I had the stalwart faith to start a gratitude list in those first months after Dan's death. I did thank God in my journal and prayers, but it was haphazard, and I spent way more time begging God for help than looking for marks of his help.

No, I stumbled onto intentional gratitude. At some point, I was simply desperate enough to hunt for God's goodness in a life gone bad, so I began starting my daily Bible time with thanks instead of rushing into prayer requests. I opened my journal, numbered seven lines down the left-hand side of the page, and thinking back over the day before, recorded my thanks. Here's day one of my gratitude list:

1. Seven healthy children.
2. Money from selling the books to repair the roof.
3. The mallard duck couple I saw this morning.
4. Your forgiveness when I mess up royally.
5. Ben taking Matt fishing.
6. An engineering club for Seth.
7. A youth pastor who loves my kids.

Each day, I'd add to the list:

8. A good day with the kids.
9. Michelle texting that Scripture just when I needed it.
10. Time to work on the bar exam.
11. An invitation to Lifeworks at the River Club.
12. My sweet girl who loves pink and flowers.
13. Health insurance.
14. Dinner around the table.

As I stumbled into gratitude, I discovered its secret gift: The more we intentionally stop to thank God for what he's doing in the hard, the more we'll see him doing in the hard.

Cultivating gratitude helped me connect the dots between my prayers and God's answers. And as I began to see evidence of God's goodness all around me, in little and big ways, I began to see how my feelings might catch up with the truth: Life could be good again.

The more we intentionally stop to thank God for what he's doing in the hard, the more we'll see him doing in the hard.

What I know now, after eight years of near-daily thanks, is that God's goodness is never a before and after. No moment or day can divide us from God's goodness. It doesn't start and stop. It is continuously immeasurable, and it is up to us to open our eyes to see it.

My only regret in cultivating gratitude is not starting sooner. I would have seen the neon signs of God's personal and practical goodness all around me. Maybe, like I did, you're wondering how you can give thanks when life feels so hard. Or maybe your thanks, like my early journal pages, is haphazard and offered only when God does something big for you. Let me show you what I found about giving thanks in all things—good and bad.

How Can We Give Thanks in Bad Circumstances?

First Thessalonians 5:18 tells us, "Give thanks in all circumstances; for this is God's will for you in Christ Jesus."

How can we give thanks in devastating disappointment? How can we give thanks when the person who pledged lifelong love has capitulated and pledged that love to someone else? How can we give thanks when the economy cripples the business we labored and sacrificed over? What about when our child is dealing with a condition we can't fix, or we're diagnosed with a chronic condition that steals the life we planned?

Does 1 Thessalonians 5:18 mean we're to thank God for cancer or drunk drivers or broken dreams? No. We're not commanded to be thankful for evil. God doesn't call us to give thanks *for* everything, but to give thanks *in* everything. Even in life-shattering loss and disappointment. Because even in the worst circumstances, God is powerfully at work. Even in the worst circumstances, we can trace God's mercy. And even in the worst circumstances, if we open our eyes, we will see the good God is doing right in our midst.

God doesn't call us to give thanks* for *everything, but to give thanks* in *everything.

Three years ago, in that glorious lull between Christmas and New Year's Day, I kicked back my La-Z-Boy chair and opened my laptop to start a new writing project. My college son, Seth, walked in the back door after his last day at work before moving to the university he'd dreamed about attending since he was a young boy. He said his back hurt.

"Go get a hot shower and see if that helps" was my mom advice.

But a few minutes later, he emerged from his room, now crying and saying he needed to go to the emergency room. When your twenty-year-old sports-loving son says his back hurts enough to go to the ER, you close the laptop and go.

After an inconclusive ER visit and some pain meds, I made an appointment with a family doctor for the next day. That doctor thought it was pulled muscles from a bad golf swing and ordered an MRI. I accelerated the MRI because Seth was supposed to be starting spring classes soon.

Early the next morning, my cell phone buzzed. It's rarely good when the doctor calls on a Saturday. The MRI showed a lemon-sized mass on Seth's lower spine. Seth had been in grueling pain, and it was getting worse. He was unable to sleep or get any comfort from pain medication, and now we knew why. But we wouldn't know anything more until we could get to the neurosurgeon on Monday.

After telling Seth as gently as possible what the MRI showed, I got into the shower. My world seemed to be closing in on me again. A host of possible scenarios and fears cascaded through my thoughts, and tears flowed freely. In the midst of paralyzing fear, the practice of cultivating gratitude saved me. Though we were facing scary unknowns again, I realized giving thanks to God in everything meant I could thank him in advance for what I did know.

So I kneeled down under the spray of the hot shower and began thanking him.

Thank you that you will provide every need in this.
Thank you that you hold our tomorrow and the next day.
Thank you that you love Seth more than I ever could.
Thank you that you will walk with us in this.
Thank you that you have the wisdom we need to find answers for this.

Where fear had been unraveling me, I realized God's supernatural peace now steadied me. I would make Seth as comfortable as possible over the weekend and find a neurosurgeon to see him first thing Monday. I could give you so many details about how God tenderly took care of Seth through this—how we got an appointment on Monday when there were no appointments, how Seth got into surgery the next day because of two patient no-shows (who doesn't show up for neurosurgery?), how our pastor arrived to pray with us just as Seth was being wheeled in for surgery, how a friend in my Sunday school class happened to be the pre-op nurse, how the university changed Seth to a full online schedule in one phone call, and how his proton radiation physician specialized in his particular tumor.

In the end, we learned the tumor encapsulated in Seth's spinal sac had burst, causing the tremendous pain. Though he was frighteningly close to permanent nerve damage, the surgery was successful and the tumor, though serious, was benign. Seth was able to return to classes at his dream university and undergo proton radiation in our hometown the next summer. Everything I had thanked God for in advance, I witnessed him do in real time.

I also saw God's goodness in a hundred ways on the day Dan died. God did not answer my prayer to preserve Dan's life, but God's goodness was all around me. It was his goodness to prompt me earlier that week to go with Dan on his business trip to the Florida Keys for four rare, beautiful days alone. It was God's goodness that Dan died at home, not on our trip, not at work, not while driving with our kids in the car. It was God's goodness a friend happened to be at her mountain home near the camp where my son Ben was a counselor, and she drove over to be with him when I told him his dad had died.

It was God's goodness that a dear friend got to the hospital in those dark morning hours before I did and held my hand as the doctor told me they were unable to revive Dan. It was God's goodness when my door opened again and again that day as family, friends, and neighbors came to be with us. It was God's goodness as I listened to my teens and their friends upstairs working through this tragedy with guitars and praise songs. It was God's goodness when friends took over tasks of notifying extended family, ordering plane tickets, organizing a way to get Ben home. And it was God's goodness to go before us exactly one year earlier to prompt Dan, who was young and had not been sick, to write out requests for his funeral one day: song requests, Scripture, his testimony, and even what special food to serve. Those are just a few good things we witnessed.

Whether we get a happy ending or endure a devastating loss, giving thanks helps us see that God has not abandoned us. Giving thanks in everything lifts our eyes off our circumstances and helps us see that, even in the hard, God is ruling in all the ways—big and little—and he cares for us. Giving thanks in everything helps us hold on to hope that though life doesn't feel good, God is.

The Cost of Thanklessness

God doesn't suggest that we become thankful; he commands it. Take a look at these verses:

> Enter his gates with thanksgiving and his courts with praise; give thanks to him and praise his name.
>
> Psalm 100:4

> Sing and make music from your heart to the Lord, **always giving thanks to God the Father for everything.**
>
> Ephesians 5:19–20, emphasis added

> So then, just as you received Christ Jesus as Lord, continue to live your lives in him . . . **overflowing with thankfulness.**
>
> Colossians 2:6–7, emphasis added

> Let the peace of Christ rule in your hearts, since as members of one body you were called to peace. **And be thankful.** . . . And whatever you do, whether in word or deed, do it all in the name of the Lord Jesus, **giving thanks to God the Father through him.**
>
> Colossians 3:15, 17, emphasis added

Both an attitude of gratitude and an attitude of ingratitude reflect what we really believe about God.

When we express gratitude, we reflect beliefs about God like these:

Both an attitude of gratitude and an attitude of ingratitude reflect what we really believe about God.

- You are good and you do good.
- Your path for me is good.
- You are a God of abundance.
- You provide all I need; what I don't have, I don't need right now.
- You are enough. Your grace is sufficient.
- You are Creator and I am created. You are the Potter and I am the clay.

What does ingratitude reflect about our belief in God?

- You are good only when life feels good.
- I know better than you what is good for me.
- You are withholding good from me.
- You should give me my wants as well as my needs.
- You and what you do for me aren't enough.
- I reject what you have allowed for me.

Ingratitude rears its unsightly head in the first chapters of the Bible. We often note Adam and Eve rebelled against God because of their pride and covetousness, but there was also ingratitude.

Genesis 1 tells us God created the world, declaring it good. On the sixth day, God created Adam and Eve and blessed them—and then he gave. He gave Adam and Eve every single plant and tree for their epicurean delight except one: God commanded them not to eat of the Tree of Knowledge of Good and Evil, because if they ate of it, they would die.[1]

Sounds easy. They didn't have to plant, till, weed, wait, or haul water to the garden, nor did they have to traipse through the woods hunting something for dinner. God had given them breath, abundant food, complete safety, endless days warmed by the sun, nights under a canopy of stars, time to explore and enjoy the vast creation, perfect health, a marriage made by heaven, and intimacy with God. What more could they want?

There is always something more we can want.

Into this idyllic garden slithered Satan, who approached Eve with a question: "Did God really say, 'You must not eat from any tree in the garden'?"[2]

The enemy had planted his own garden with seeds of discontent, causing Eve to question God and his goodness. Eve replied to the serpent with a half-truth: "God did say, 'You must not eat fruit from the tree that is in the middle of the garden, and you must not touch it, or you will die.'"[3] Her answer wasn't true: They could look, touch, climb on, and sit under the shade of that tree all they wanted. God had commanded only that Adam and Eve not eat from it.

The serpent pressed the discontent button a little harder with a bold-faced lie: "You will not certainly die. . . . For God knows that when you eat from it your eyes will be opened, and you will be like God, knowing good and evil."[4] In that lie, Satan wanted Eve to believe God was withholding good from her.

That's when Eve caved. "When the woman saw that the fruit of the tree was good for food and pleasing to the eye, and also desirable for gaining wisdom, she took some and ate it. She also gave some to her husband, who was with her, and he ate it" (Genesis 3:6).

Instead of turning off Satan's lies that God had withheld good from them, and instead of turning to God in deep thankfulness for all he had given them, Adam and Eve focused on the one thing in the whole garden they didn't have.

Instead of trusting God was good and did only good for them, they believed God was capable of goodness but had withheld it from them.

Both an attitude of gratitude and an attitude of ingratitude reflect what we really believe about God.

Let's stop and take our own gratitude pulse. Let's assess whether we have any hidden areas of ingratitude in our current struggles. As you read through this list, mentally place a mark (or use that pen!) on the line of each statement to show what you believe right now:

I trust God is good even though I don't feel good right now.	I doubt God's goodness because I don't feel good right now.
I know God has good for my future even though I can't see it yet.	I believe everything good is behind me.
I believe God is a God of abundance, not scarcity.	I think God has withheld good from me.
I trust God is in control even though my circumstances are shaking.	I am doubting God's control because my circumstances are shaking.
I trust God will provide what I need when I need it.	I have asked for God to meet my needs and he hasn't come through.
I am content even if God never gives me what I prayed for.	I cannot truly be happy unless I get what I prayed for.
I don't like what's happened, but I see God's goodness for me.	I reject what God has allowed, and I see little or none of God's goodness for me.

This isn't a pass/fail quiz. It's an opportunity to take an honest look at our hearts and see where we've allowed ingratitude to take up space and where we've bought the enemy's lie that God can't be trusted because he's taken something good from us. And then to root out the ingratitude that blinds us to the truth.

The truth is God is good even when circumstances aren't what we wanted.

The truth is God is good to us even when life feels bad.

The truth is God is working his good right now even if we can't yet see.

These words by Winston Smith show how apt we are to miss God's kindness:

> God knows how often we fail to recognize the ways that he's caring for us, how often we even mistake his care for neglect, wrath, or rejection. Like the Israelites, we misinterpret his gracious provision of manna and water not as help for those being rescued, but as bread and water slid beneath the cell door to those he's imprisoned. When we fail to locate God's love and care in the details of our lives, our hearts begin to get hard. We begin to misinterpret our circumstances, our lives, and God himself. Before long, we're accusing the Good Shepherd of being a nasty tyrant. Unchecked we risk losing sight of God's love altogether.[5]

Oh, friend, I know choosing gratitude is hard when you feel like everyone around you is getting the life they ordered and you feel stuck in a life you didn't. But when we choose gratitude in the midst of difficulty, we defy the enemy.

Choosing gratitude aligns our heart to the truth that God never has and never will withhold good from us.

> For the Lord God is a sun and shield; the Lord bestows favor and honor; no good thing does he withhold from those whose walk is blameless.
>
> Psalm 84:11

The Power of Gratitude

God doesn't need our thanksgiving. Revelation tells us God is right now surrounded by creatures giving him constant thanksgiving.[6]

So then, why does God tell us to give thanks in every circumstance? Because we need it. God knows the power of gratitude for us. Let's look at six benefits when we cultivate thankfulness.

1. **Gratitude helps us see God's hand and opens our spiritual eyes.** There's a beautiful cycle I found when we give God thanks: The more we thank him, the more we see him working in us and around us. Gratitude helps us sense God's presence, his personal care, and his perfect timing.

   > Do not be deceived, my beloved brothers. Every good gift and every perfect gift is from above, coming down from the Father of lights.
   >
   > James 1:16–17 ESV

2. **Gratitude draws us to God.** As we begin to regularly thank God for what he's doing, we draw closer to him. Seeing God's kindness to us day in and day out softens our heart and woos us to him. We see this benefit of gratitude in the narrative of Jesus healing ten lepers. When they begged for healing, Jesus told them to go

to the priests for cleansing. All ten went because all ten wanted healing. But only one wanted the Healer. That one turned back, fell at Jesus' feet, and gave thanks.

> Jesus replied, "Weren't ten men healed? Where are the other nine? No one returned to praise God except this foreigner?" Then Jesus said to him, "Get up and go. Your faith has healed you."
>
> Luke 17:17–19 CEB

3. **Gratitude helps us trade worry for peace.** We trade our worry for his peace when we pray *with thanksgiving*. Our tendency is to give our concerns to God and ask him to fix them. But God tells us to give him our requests along with thanks, and he will give us supernatural peace.

> Don't be anxious about anything; rather, bring up all of your requests to God in your prayers and petitions, along with giving thanks. Then the peace of God that exceeds all understanding will keep your hearts and minds safe in Christ Jesus.
>
> Philippians 4:6–7 CEB

4. **Gratitude deepens our faith.** When we stop to remember what God has done and thank him for it, our faith deepens. In the busyness of our days, we can easily miss how God personally and practically answers our prayers and meets our needs. Giving thanks—better yet, recording our thanks in an app or journal—helps us connect the dots. We can go back months or years later and see a continuous record of God's faithfulness.

That's why God commanded Israel to remember his great deeds.

> Remember how the Lord your God led you all the way in the wilderness these forty years, to humble and test you in order to know what was in your heart, whether or not you would keep his commands.
>
> Deuteronomy 8:2

5. **Gratitude gives joy.** Gratitude is the gateway to joy and helps us find contentment right where we are. Gratitude opens our eyes to the countless blessings in our life and helps us appreciate the ordinary beauty we would otherwise pass by. And gratitude turns struggles, annoyances, and disappointments inside out by helping us see God's mercies laced through them.

> When the Lord restored the fortunes of Zion, we were like those who dreamed. Our mouths were filled with laughter, our tongues with songs of joy. . . . The Lord has done great things for us, and we are filled with joy.
>
> Psalm 126:1–3

6. **Gratitude silences Satan's lies.** Satan knows the power of gratitude for us and would love nothing more than to keep us ungrateful. When we give thanks, we muzzle the lies Satan whispers that God is keeping good from us. We see instead that God is an abundant God who gives lavishly to us.

> If you, then, though you are evil, know how to give good gifts to your children, how much more will

> your Father in heaven give good gifts to those who ask him!
>
> Matthew 7:11

A thankful heart doesn't just happen. We're much more prone to grumbling than gratitude, which is why we need to intentionally cultivate gratitude. How? I have two favorite ways.

The first is to make a 100 List. Pull out a piece of lined paper or open a spiral notebook and number the lines 1 to 100. Then, in one sitting, begin writing what you're thankful for. As you get down the list and move through the obvious and big things, you'll have to reflect and remember more deeply to get to one hundred. Then you'll realize you could keep going to two hundred and three hundred because God has given abundantly to you. The 100 List is an eye-opening, soul-expanding exercise.

But my favorite way to cultivate gratitude is to keep a daily list. Get a journal or use the Notes app in your phone and begin to record five to seven things you can thank God for each day. It's a daily pause to capture what God is doing and how he's working, and a forever record of God's goodness through every circumstance.

A Prayer of Gratitude

Lord, forgive me for my thanklessness. Forgive me for not stopping to thank you for who you are and all you have done. You are good and you do good. Thank you for saving me and giving me your righteousness. Thank you for keeping me from what I wanted that would have harmed me. Thank you for your provision and presence in this hard place. Thank you in advance for all you will do. Open my eyes to all you are doing and give me a heart of deep gratitude. In Jesus' name, amen.

8

Crush Your Fear

But blessed is the one who trusts in the Lord, whose confidence is in him. They will be like a tree planted by the water that sends out its roots by the stream. It does not fear when heat comes; its leaves are always green. It has no worries in a year of drought and never fails to bear fruit.

Jeremiah 17:7–8

Until we get to the point we see what our fears have cost us, we will not hate them enough to let them go.

Lisa Whittle

When the unthinkable happens, it swings the door wide open to all manner of new fears. Before Dan died, I could brush off most of my fears as being farfetched; they would probably never happen. And of all the things I feared, Dan dying in his forties wasn't one of them. It wasn't even in the realm of possible scenarios. But then, without a single visible symptom or any kind of warning whatsoever, my husband had a fatal heart attack on an ordinary Friday morning while sleeping on the pillow next to mine. What we didn't know then was that he had an underlying problem, a ticking time bomb we had no idea would one day go off.

After Dan's death, vague what-ifs suddenly became paralyzing fears that no longer seemed farfetched. The unthinkable can and does happen, and my life was proof. I was ambushed by fear with a slew of all-new worries. I couldn't begin to imagine what might happen next. Every single expectation and all my plans for the future had been centered in my marriage. Looking ahead was like straining to see into a black hole. I couldn't begin to fathom what kind of life there could be for me in a year or five.

Finances were another worry. I knew in the short term we were okay, but Dan was the sole breadwinner for our family. Neither of us had planned on me going back to work, and I'd formally retired as an attorney years before. Going back to work meant taking the Florida bar exam all over again. We had some life insurance, but now it sure seemed like we should have bought more. I worried about having enough to raise seven children and get them through college, plus my own long-term security.

I was terrified for my children. I'd long heard of the dismal statistics of children raised without a father in the home. Plus, I knew a couple of families where a parent's death had caused one of the kids to spiral dangerously downward. I worried about my teen boys who needed the strong spine, wisdom, and example of a father to get them to manhood. I worried for Matt, who was only six when Dan died and just beginning to identify with his dad. I cringed when I thought of Annalise at four years old, growing up with almost no memories of her dad. I worried for my teen daughter facing lifelong decisions without her father.

There were other fears: As the sole parent, I worried something could happen to me. My stomach churned over having to figure out what to do with a rental house that needed hands-on attention and another that needed so many repairs I didn't know where to start.

Then the catastrophizing began. Catastrophizing is imagining and then practically expecting worst-case scenarios.

Something had to change because fear had frozen my ability to move forward.

What Fear Steals

Fear is a stronghold, and it's especially pernicious when life has turned upside down. Jesus tells us in John 10:10 that the "thief comes only to steal and kill and destroy; I have come that they may have life, and have it to the full." The devil knows how destructive fear is. While we may have dealt with garden variety fear before, the emotions and upheaval that come when life implodes make us especially vulnerable.

Fear steals so much from us—like joy. We can never experience true joy or delight in the life God has for us if underneath we're consumed with worry. In fact, fear will cut joy off at the start by convincing us we'll never be happy again and life will never be as good as it once was.

Fear also steals our peace. It keeps our mind churning over the what-ifs and our hands wringing over the what-might-bes so that we're unable to rest in God's sovereignty. In the midst of change and a host of unknowns about our present and future, we desperately need peace. Instead of stirred up and fretting, we need to be steadied by the peace God has for us.

Finally, fear steals our ability to move forward. It immobilizes us because we're too afraid to make a wrong decision and too scared to do new, hard things. Fear can make us withdraw so much we become isolated and won't let others help or walk with us in the hard places. It cripples us and keeps us from taking the hard steps needed to move through disappointment and embrace life as it is now.

In some ways, the enormous fear I had after Dan died was as hard to deal with as the pain of missing him. I needed to parent well, I needed to process the emotions of loss, and I wanted to live life fully again, but I couldn't do it carrying the oppressive weight of fear.

The breakthrough came one morning over coffee with my friend Teresa. She and I go a long way back. We've swapped kids for slumber parties, led book clubs and debate clubs, and talked through many a thorny parenting problem. She was the friend I called to meet me at the emergency room in the dark early morning after Dan was taken by ambulance.

Teresa knows what it is to face fear and to be utterly dependent on God. For more than two decades, she's battled multiple sclerosis with incredible faith and courage. She knows all too well how fear and worry can steal the joy and goodness of life now if we let them.

Somewhere in our conversation over coffee that morning, as hot tears spilled down my cheeks, I told Teresa how anxious I was, especially for my kids. Teresa is a great listener, but when I started talking about my fear, she sat up.

She'd been through this, and she shared a verse that has become a key to winning against worry.

Three Steps to Beating Fear

"Oh, I know this one," Teresa said. And she began to quote 2 Corinthians 10:

> For though we live in the world, we do not wage war as the world does. The weapons we fight with are not the weapons of the world. On the contrary, they have divine power to demolish strongholds. We demolish arguments and every pretension that sets itself up against the knowledge of God, and we take captive every thought to make it obedient to Christ.
>
> vv. 3–5

The war against fear is fought and won in our mind. Most of our fear isn't based on present danger but on possibility, and most of those possibilities are highly remote. Worry dwells on fear, letting it grow bigger and bigger and take up more and more space in our thoughts. Anxiety is worry that shows up physically—in stomachaches, migraines, chest tightening, or sleepless hours spent tossing and turning. The root of it all is in our mind.

The war against fear is fought and won in our mind.

God has given us a practical three-step process for overcoming fear in 2 Corinthians 10:3–5. The first step is to identify the stronghold of fear. The second step is to call out the lie behind the fear that sets itself up against the knowledge of God. And the third step is to take captive every thought and make it obedient to Christ. We can crush the crippling fear by replacing lies from the enemy with truth from God.

We've already seen the stronghold that fear has over us, and the joy, peace, and progress the enemy steals from us through fear. The next step, then, is to identify the fear that grips our thoughts. Sometimes that fear manifests in anger or withdrawal, edginess with others, or procrastinating rather than doing things we need to do. Fear often shows up when we're parenting from a place of fear, responding out of fear, or paralyzed by fear.

Once we've recognized our fear, the second step is to call out the lie behind it. Every fear is based on a lie from the enemy. In her book *Fierce Faith*, Alli Worthington says that fear "speaks over us so convincingly, we believe that something terrible is certain to happen, even in the absence of any evidence whatsoever. Fear turns our what-ifs into certainties, freezing our faith and flipping our world upside down."[1]

For example, our fear for the future might be based on the lie that we're overdue for a bad event. Parenting fears can be based on the lie that a child's isolated bad behavior means they're destined for a life of bad behavior. Our financial fears are often based on the lie that God can't or won't provide for us.

When one of our fears flares up and we've identified the lie behind it, the third step is to take it captive with God's truth. As I dealt with my fears, I imagined a lasso encircling the lie and pulling it from my thoughts, making room for the truth of God. How do we know God's truth? We find it in God's promises and his character. That's why it's so important to be in God's Word consistently, to let God's truth continually wash over us so we can use it against the lies of fear.

Here's how I applied 2 Corinthians 10:3–5 to my fear of raising kids in a single-parent home. First, I identified the fear that had become a stronghold—that my kids might act out because of deep grief. Next, I called out the lie behind the fear. Yes, there were troublesome statistics from single-mom families, and yes, I knew kids who spiraled downward after a parent passed away. But I don't live by statistics, and you probably don't either. If we did, we'd never get on the highways that crisscross our cities. While I knew other kids who acted out in deep grief, I didn't know their whole story or all the variables at play in those families.

Finally, I needed to replace those lies with God's truth, and I went hunting for it in Scripture. Using the concordance in my Bible, I looked up every verse on widows and the fatherless. As I studied, I was amazed that God's Word covered this season I never saw coming, and that verses I had once skimmed were now truth over my family. I penned the date next to many verses and began to form a full picture of how God cares for the widow—the single mom—and the fatherless. Here are a few of these verses:

- "A father to the fatherless, a defender of widows, is God in his holy dwelling" (Psalm 68:5).
- "He defends the cause of the fatherless and the widow" (Deuteronomy 10:18).
- "But I will protect the orphans who remain among you. Your widows, too, can depend on me for help" (Jeremiah 49:11 NLT).

My fears were unfounded. God's Word assures us over and over that he specifically cares for us. We would walk through pain, but God himself would be Father to my children. Every single thing they had depended on their earthly father for—protection, provision, guidance, and more—God promised to provide if they looked to him for it.

Where are you seeing lies that you need to replace with God's truth right now? Why does it seem easier to dwell on the fears than to look to God to wipe out our fears with his faithfulness?

I was able to crush the stronghold of this particular fear by replacing it with God's specific truth. But that crushing wasn't a one-and-done process; it was ongoing. Each time this fear reared up, I'd call out the lie and silently recite the promise in one of those verses. Eventually, the power of God's truth was enough to extinguish that particular fear altogether, especially as I saw God taking care of us personally and practically just as he'd promised.

When we replace lies with God's truth, we begin to see how God is taking care of us and those we love right here, right now.

Getting to the Root of Fear

There's another taproot of fear, and that is me: my comfort, my expectations, my agenda, my entitlement. So often, when I dig under the fear, I realize I've elevated some person, place, or event higher than Almighty God. The idols underlying my fear stand out in relief against this rock-bottom truth: This life isn't about me, and this life isn't all there is.

If the goals of my life are grounded in gathering and getting, I'm going to fear losing it. If the goals of my life are grounded in my comfort, I'm going to fear any interruption. If the goals of my life are grounded in my position, I'm going to fear rejection. If the goals of my life are grounded in my agenda, I'm going to fear anything that hinders my dreams. If my goal is to live well into old age, I'm going to fear anything that would shorten my days.

God has given us breath today for one purpose: to glorify him. That's it. We wake up today not to get more or be seen more or do more, but to give him more. Any other goal is an idol we've put on a throne above God. And that idol stirs up a protective fear. The cotton candy Christianity of today encourages me to think that as a believer trying my best to obey God, I'm entitled to a great house, a dream job, long health, and days of ease. Clinging to anything else more tightly than we're clinging to God's glory triggers the fear of losing it.

We can lose an idol we've carved; we can never lose God.

We can lose an idol we've carved; we can never lose God.

Fear keeps us in bondage to acquire more. God gives us strength to trust him and live with less. Less stress, less worry, and less of our ability to control the outcome when he already knows it.

If our life is centered on glorifying God alone, then fear has no legs. Because no matter what happens—with our health, with our money, with our jobs, with our families—no matter what, we can glorify God in each of these areas.

What about your fear? What lies are fomenting that fear? What truths from God do you need planted bone deep to uproot the lies trying to steal, kill, and destroy life from you right now? God's Word is sufficient to shut down any lie the enemy whispers to you.

In appendix A, I've gathered forty promises of God. Use this list of promises or search the Scriptures using one of the online Bible search tools to find verses you need right now to fight your fear. Write those verses down and pull them out when fear rears its head. Every time that fear crops up, call it out as a lie from the enemy, and take it captive with God's truth.

> I sought the LORD, and he answered me; he delivered me from all my fears.
>
> Psalm 34:4

God is with you. I'm here to declare this deep truth. If not, we would have no hope. But since we have found ourselves in a place where we must trust, let's hold strongly to the truth that God alone is worthy of our trust. We won't give it to another person, a job, a bank statement, or anything else that draws our focus from the one true God.

A Prayer against Fear

Dear Lord, I am paralyzed by my fear. I have to do things that are far too big for me, and I am facing a future with far too many unknowns. I am worried about ____________, but this fear is based on a lie that says ____________, so I take that lie captive to your truth that says ____________. Lord, help me to root out this fear that I might live out the abundant joy and peace you have for me. In Jesus' name, amen.

9

The Enemy in the Midst of This

> "Simon, Simon, Satan has asked to sift each of you like wheat."
>
> Luke 22:31 NLT

> His enemies had counted on the lions taking care of Daniel. What they hadn't counted on was his God taking care of Daniel.
>
> Tony Evans

Satan works his hardest when we're at our weakest.

Truth is, the enemy is always working against us. We're in a spiritual battle because you and I are breathing, not because of our circumstances. When life is going along as planned and we're pretty comfortable, the enemy lulls us into forgetting that a spiritual battle rages around us. But come to a season of deep pain or a wilderness of disappointment, and you can almost see the enemy's fiery arrows flying furiously toward you.

When life falls apart, one of the biggest battles isn't processing the emotions of deep loss or handling all the decisions, as hard as those are. One of the biggest battles is spiritual. It's surprising, actually. We're giving it everything we've got to show up for the day when *bam!* In comes a low slug from the enemy.

Satan has a history of kicking us when we're down. When circumstances feel like they're going to crush us, the enemy would love nothing more than to finish the job. He comes to steal, kill, and destroy—steal our peace, kill our hope, and destroy any semblance of the abundant life God has promised us.

I'll be the first to admit that talking about the devil isn't on my list of favorite things to do. I'd rather keep the conversation light and upbeat. I'd much rather speak to the goodness of God than the evil of Satan. But ignoring spiritual warfare doesn't make it go away. Instead, it leaves us unprepared and vulnerable. God has given us every single tool we need not just to fight the enemy, but to overcome the enemy. We don't need to fear him or fear thinking about him. As we'll see in this chapter, God has utterly defeated Satan on our behalf.

The enemy comes to steal our peace, kill our hope, and destroy any semblance of the abundant life God has promised us.

It may feel like you're fighting a diagnosis, a lack of finances, loneliness, an ex-spouse, a boss, or even someone under your own roof. But that's not your real enemy. The real enemy is always Satan.

> For we do not wrestle against flesh and blood, but against the rulers, against the authorities, against the cosmic powers over

> this present darkness, against the spiritual forces of evil in the heavenly places.
>
> Ephesians 6:12 ESV

The Phillips translation says it like this: "For our fight is not against any physical enemy: it is against organisations and powers that are spiritual. We are up against the unseen power that controls this dark world, and spiritual agents from the very headquarters of evil."

So let's unmask the real enemy we're up against. He may not be visible to us, but Scripture tells us everything we need to know about him. Let's start with some of his names to get an idea of who he is. Here are a few:

- Satan, a Hebrew word meaning "adversary" or "opponent," stemming from a Hebrew word meaning "to oppose or attack."
- Devil, meaning one who slanders, falsely accuses, defames, "[makes] charges that bring down," and destroys.[1]
- Adversary, a legal term for an opponent at court, seeking to exact a binding penalty.[2]
- Tempter, one who solicits or entices to sin.[3]
- The accuser of the brethren, from the Hebrew, meaning prosecutor, who day and night stands before God accusing believers.[4]

Satan is not some passive couch potato, sending out hate thoughts toward you. He is active, personal, and strategic. This is spiritual *war*. Not target practice, not laser tag, but all-out war, where Satan comes at you with one goal—to destroy. He wants to destroy you, your family, your ministry, your marriage, your faith.

New Circumstances, Same Old Tactics

You may be facing a new struggle, but the enemy's tactics are antique. Ephesians 6:11 warns us of Satan's schemes. The word *schemes* is *methodeias* in Greek, which means a "predictable (pre-set) method used in organized evil-doing (well-crafted) trickery."[5] Satan twists truth to undermine our faith. He lies to accuse and discourage us, leaving us feeling defeated, ashamed, and devalued. Jesus said he "was a murderer from the beginning, not holding to the truth, for there is no truth in him. When he lies, he speaks his native language, for he is a liar and the father of lies" (John 8:44).

He also tempts us to sin and actively rebel against God. We saw that with Adam and Eve in chapter 7. First Peter 5:8 tells us the "devil prowls around like a roaring lion looking for someone to devour."

Think of that: As I write this and as you read it, the enemy is prowling around both of us like a predatory lion, positioning to pounce with claws and jaws eager to destroy.

And like a lion stalking its prey, Satan often comes at us when we're already overwhelmed with life's unexpected moments, and when hard days leave us physically, mentally, and emotionally depleted. Satan seizes his opportunity.

Look at how Satan came at Jesus in the wilderness.

In Luke 4, the Holy Spirit led Jesus into the wilderness, where Jesus fasted for forty days and nights, to be tempted by the devil. Satan didn't come on day one or day two or even day ten of that fast. The devil came on day forty. Jesus was hungry and Satan came offering bread. Three times Satan tempted Jesus with a twisted lie, and each time Jesus countered with God's truth. Jesus may have been physically weak, but he drew spiritual strength from the Word. And Satan can never stand against the truth of Scripture.

Luke then adds this important detail: "When the devil had finished all this tempting, he left him until an opportune time" (Luke 4:13). The Greek word meaning "opportune time"—*kairos*—refers to circumstances "coming to a head to take full advantage of."[6] Satan wasn't done. Not by a long shot. He was just waiting for the next opportune time to attack again.

That same enemy prowls around you and me, waiting to take full advantage of our physical, emotional, and mental weakness. His attacks often come back-to-back-to-back, wearing us down with each turn. When life is already hard enough and our emotions are already fragile, the enemy's attacks create serious battle fatigue.

But we were never meant to fight these battles on our own. The enemy attacks, but God is offense, defense, and commander. It's not even a fair fight. God isn't Satan's sparring equal, because while Satan has limited authority, God has limitless power. "Satan is a lion," David Platt writes," but he's a lion on a leash. And God holds the leash."[7]

This is super fresh for me because even as I was writing this chapter, Satan was hard at work. I'd been clipping along with my writing until I hit this one on spiritual warfare, and all the words and energy left me. I got discouraged by insecurities like *I don't know enough* and *I haven't researched enough*. I got distracted by menial tasks that should have waited. I paused way too often to check Facebook and Instagram. The longer I scrolled, the more disheartened I became. *Who am I to write? What was I thinking?* I closed my laptop and turned in for the day, vowing to dig in harder next time.

After two weekends of this, I realized what was going on. How could I have missed the enemy's discouragement and distraction when I was writing on it? If this meant war, I had my own strategy.

I copied Ephesians 6:14–19 onto a sticky note, listing each spiritual weapon and personalizing it for this project, naming how each weapon defeated Satan. Then I stuck the notes on my car window. I was writing in my minivan during my daughter's all-day dance practice. Finally, I bathed it in prayer and asked a couple friends to battle for me in prayer as well.

And with God's truth literally surrounding me, I finally found the focus and words needed to push forward and write. Let's look at these spiritual weapons God gives us to overcome Satan's schemes.

Your Powerful Arsenal

Becoming a boy mom has meant becoming okay with weapons. My sons have studied, made, collected, and used all manner of play and real weapons as they've grown from boys to men. At four years old, one of them nearly memorized a thick book on medieval weapons and could tell me the difference between a catapult and trebuchet, a battle-axe and a mace. They had a small armory of popguns, longbows, wooden swords, battle-axes, and cowboy pistols, and they spent hours enacting battles and ambushes in the woods behind our house. Their dad taught them how to safely use a pocketknife while fishing and a shotgun for hunting, and even after their dad died, I felt pretty safe with five boys who knew how to use weapons.

We have an armory as well. Ephesians 6:10–19 describes our seven pieces of spiritual armor. As you read this passage, note each piece of armor and what it's used for.

> Finally, be strong in the Lord and in his mighty power. Put on the full armor of God, that you can take your stand against the devil's schemes. . . . Therefore put on the full armor of God, so

> that when the day of evil comes, you may be able to stand your ground, and after you have done everything, to stand. Stand firm then, with the belt of truth buckled around your waist, with the breastplate of righteousness in place, and with your feet fitted with the readiness that comes from the gospel of peace. In addition to all this, take up the shield of faith, with which you can extinguish all the flaming arrows of the evil one. Take the helmet of salvation and the sword of the Spirit, which is the word of God. And pray in the Spirit on all occasions with all kinds of prayers and requests. . . . Always keep on praying.
>
> Ephesians 6:10–11, 13–18

Three times, this passage assures us that our spiritual armor enables us to stand firm against the enemy. But we have to actively "put on" the full armor. Not some of it, because partial armor will leave us with an Achilles heel of vulnerability, and that's where the enemy will aim. Ephesians lists these pieces of armor:

The belt of truth
The breastplate of righteousness
Feet fitted with the gospel of peace
The shield of faith
The helmet of salvation
The sword of the Spirit

These sound as ancient as the weapons in the book of medieval weapons my son memorized. Our modern world doesn't provide the frame of reference those in the Roman and Greek worlds who received this letter would have had. Yet they are just as applicable to us today as then. Let's look at each piece of armor and how we use it against the devil.

Our belt of truth. I don't use belts (hello, post-baby figure), but I sure love the look of a slim leather belt looped through jeans. But Ephesians 6 isn't referring to a slim leather accessory. The Roman soldier wrapped his torso "with something more akin to a girdle than a belt," writes Priscilla Shirer. "The sturdy, leather girdle of the Roman soldier was made to reach around the torso and provide essential support while he performed the quick, demanding movements of war."[8]

Like the Roman soldier's girdle, God's truth supports and upholds us against the devil's lies. In spiritual warfare, being girded with God's truth is essential. Are you studying the Bible often enough to silence the enemy? Is God's voice, through his Word, the loudest voice in your day? Wrapping our mind in God's truth mutes the enemy's lies every time.

Our breastplate of righteousness. The Roman breastplate protected the soldier's torso and vital organs like the heart and lungs.

Our spiritual armor is a breastplate *of righteousness*. Putting on our own righteousness—the ability to do all the right things according to God—will fail every time. Satan not only tempts us to do wrong, but he reminds us when we've done it. Remember one of his names means *accuser*. He loves to heap on shame and regret of past failures.

As children of God, our breastplate is the righteousness of Christ. Once we repent and trust Jesus as our Savior, we are forever clothed with God's perfect righteousness, and nothing the enemy says can change it. Whenever the enemy launches his arrows of shame and condemnation, are you letting them hit deep or are you deflecting them with the truth of God's righteousness? One verse that I've learned to have on repeat when shame creeps up is Romans 8:1: "Therefore, there is now no condemnation for those who are in Christ Jesus." Take that, accuser.

Feet fitted with readiness of the gospel of peace. This always puzzled me until I learned the Roman soldiers' shoes were studded with short nails, providing stability in combat. It reminds me of the shoes two of my sons wore for high school track. The spikes on the soles of their shoes gave them the traction and stability they needed as they ran.

Boy, do we need stability when life hits us with the unexpected. The enemy doesn't want us to find our footing again and will use this "opportune time" to keep us shaken and unsettled. "He is the lord of chaos and confusion, using every opportunity to upset your sense of well-being and stability," writes Priscilla Shirer. "He wants you uneasy, unbalanced, filled with anxiety, worry, and turmoil."[9]

Our defense is spiritual footwear fit with the readiness of the gospel of peace. That's a mouthful, so let's break it down. The Greek word translated "readiness" means "foundation, firm footing; preparation, readiness."[10] Because of the gospel, we have peace with God and the peace of God. We have peace with God because Jesus' death on the cross paid the penalty for our sin, restoring our full relationship with God. As a result, we have the peace of God.

God's supernatural peace is an unshakable foundation when life shakes. We learned one practical way to access that peace in chapter 7. When you feel anxious, God says to give your needs and requests to him *with thanksgiving*, and he will give you the peace that passes understanding to protect your heart and mind.

Our shield of faith. Scripture is referencing the full-body shield used by Roman soldiers—a shield about as long as the body is tall. This shield is our faith, which Hebrews 11:1 defines as "the *assurance* of things hoped for, the *conviction* of things not seen" (ESV, emphasis added). Your shield is not some flimsy hope. The word *assurance* in the Greek literally means "standing under a guaranteed agreement" and "'title' to a promise or property."[11] Our faith stands under the guaranteed promises of God.

Listen, suffering puts our faith to the test. Grueling pain, reeling unfairness, and dreams denied can make us sit up and question God. *How could you allow this? Why would you do this? Do you even care about me?* Satan would love nothing more than to snuff out our faith and render us numb, bitter, angry, and resentful.

When the questions come and the enemy launches a full-out attack, your shield of faith—assurance that God will keep his promises though you can't yet see it—is powerful enough to quench "every burning missile the enemy hurls at you" (Ephesians 6:16 Phillips).

The helmet of salvation. No soldier goes into battle without head protection. Our thoughts influence our emotions, our choices, and our behavior. Paul tells us, "Do not conform to the pattern of this world, but be transformed by the renewing of your mind" (Romans 12:2).

Science shows the average person has 12,000 to 60,000 thoughts per day, with 80 percent of those being negative and a whopping 95 percent carried over from the day before.[12] Our minds are by nature cycling and recycling on the negative. Unless we put on our helmet of salvation.

Our spiritual helmet is not *for* salvation but *because of* salvation. Fixing our minds on the truth of God, who we are in Christ, our hope, and God's faithfulness keeps the enemy from messing with our mind.

The sword of the Spirit. The sword of the Spirit—the Word of God—is the first offensive weapon listed. When Satan came at Jesus in the wilderness with twisted lies, Jesus responded each time with the truth of Scripture. Just like the sticky notes

I posted in my minivan to get this chapter written, we need the Word always before us when the enemy is undermining us with lies.

Instagram quotes won't do it. The advice of your bestie isn't enough. Only Scripture is alive and active and powerful enough to overcome the enemy's twisted lies. Discouragement, despair, and defeat disappear when we saturate our mind with the Word.

Find a Bible reading rhythm that works for you and engage there. Maybe that's a Bible study with your local church, a livestream, or an app. Maybe it's following along with a reading plan or opening a devotional to help get you into God's Word. The Great Exchange of your thoughts for God's thoughts is powerful against the enemy.

But wait—we have one more offensive weapon.

Prayer: Your Power Source

Once again, I'm writing this from my minivan. While I have enough in me to keep writing for a while, my laptop battery only holds so much charge. When I write from home with my laptop plugged in, I have virtually unlimited power. I can write, email, and stream Zoom calls through the day, and then read an ebook or watch a movie into the evening, all from my laptop—*if* it stays plugged into the outlet.

Prayer is plugging into our power source. Talking about all this armor can make us think it's our battle to fight. While you may have grit and determination like nobody's business, let me tenderly remind you that you are no match for "the rulers . . . authorities . . . cosmic powers over this present darkness . . . spiritual forces of evil in the heavenly places" (Ephesians 6:12 ESV).

God calls us to be strong *in the Lord* and in the strength *of His might*. Our job is to make use of the spiritual armor and plug into God's power through prayer. Look how often Ephesians 6:18 says to pray: "And **pray** in the Spirit **on all occasions with all kinds of prayers and requests**. With this in mind, be alert and **always keep on praying** for all the Lord's people" (emphasis added).

Prayer connects us to God's unlimited power. Prayer fixes our mind on God's truth and anchors our faith when the enemy is taunting us to doubt. I've learned to pray for God to give me an escape when temptation comes. "Simply defined, prayer is earthly permission for heavenly interference," says author Tony Evans.[13]

Prayer is not only defensive but offensive. We don't want to simply make it through this difficulty by the skin of our teeth. We want to take back ground the enemy threatened, to be changed from the inside out and emerge more in love with God and more like Jesus than we ever were before.

We need to ask God to use what the enemy intends for evil for his good—to not just defeat Satan but bring victory.

In my own life, it's easy to see all that's missing for my children as I've single-parented. If I dwell on it, I begin to cave to fear and discouragement. I've had to learn to pray and ask God not just to help me parent but to use the very lack in our life to shape my children in ways I never could.

Can you see how the enemy has been behind your struggles all along? What if we prayed not simply to make it through this difficulty, but asked God to retake ground the enemy has stolen to use in ways we couldn't ask or imagine?

A Prayer to Win against the Enemy

Dear God, I need you to fight this battle for me. I put on the belt of truth that assures me you have equipped me to do this hard thing I'm facing. I pick up the breastplate of your righteousness that frees me from all condemnation. With shoes of peace, I ask you to steady me with your peace, and with the helmet of salvation, I declare I am your child, your beloved. With your Word, I take the lies Satan is lobbing at me captive to your truth. Give me victory over this spiritual battle to do what you've called me to do. In Jesus' name, amen.

10

Hanging On to Threadbare Hope

Against all hope, Abraham in hope believed and so became the father of many nations. . . . He did not waver through unbelief regarding the promise of God, but was strengthened in his faith and gave glory to God.

Romans 4:18, 20

We must accept finite disappointment, but never lose infinite hope.

Martin Luther King Jr.

She was at the end of her rope.

She ignored her gnawing hunger as she walked past the fish market and the baker's cart, smelling warm bread as she passed. Her mind churned on overdrive, replaying the events of the last year. Her stomach now seized with a different pain as memories of her late husband flooded in. What she would give to have those days back.

Everything changed with her husband's death. No one expected it and, really, she could have done little to prepare for it. Friends had flocked to her home, bringing food and giving condolences at the funeral. But they'd long since gone back to the chore of caring for their own families during a famine, leaving her to find her own way.

From the beginning, she rationed stores from her pantry and went without to make ends meet. Eventually, she let the household help go and sold furniture, jewelry, anything to keep bread on the table. Day after day, month after month, she found grit to keep going, to parent a growing boy through lonely grief—whatever it took to make it to the next day.

But now, she'd reached the end. There would be no next day. Brushing away hot tears, she set about with grim resolve to find firewood and get home.

As she bent to pick up a large branch, someone called to her. She looked up and saw a traveler dressed like an Israelite. She'd heard stories of the neighboring Hebrews and their Hebrew God.

"Would you bring me a little water in a jar so I may have a drink?" the stranger asked.

She nodded in acknowledgment and respect and turned to walk toward the well.

"And bring me, please, a piece of bread," he added.

His words caught her short. Turning slowly toward him, she kept her eyes on her bare feet as she answered, "I don't have any bread—only a handful of flour in a jar and a little olive oil in a jug. I am gathering a few sticks to take home to make a meal for myself and my son, that we may eat it—and die."

The despair in this young mom's words is piercing. She could see no other choice. She was out of options. Out of resources. Out of hope.

While you probably haven't had to gather wood to make a last meal, maybe you know a similar kind of hopelessness as the widow in 1 Kings 17. But hopelessness wasn't the end of this young woman's story. God was doing something that far exceeded her difficult circumstances. The stranger from Israel was none other than Elijah the prophet, whom God had sent to this destitute widow.

Though she only had enough flour and oil for one last loaf for her and her son, Elijah told her to first make bread for him.

"For this is what the Lord, the God of Israel, says," Elijah relayed. "The jar of flour will not be used up and the jug of oil will not run dry until the day the Lord sends rain on the land" (1 Kings 17:14).

This was a huge ask. Elijah was asking for all she had.

But the young widow did as Elijah instructed, and afterward, her flour jar never went empty and her oil jar never ran dry, just as God had promised. In fact, there was enough to feed the widow, her family, and Elijah throughout the entire multi-year drought.

Our world of microwaves and cell phones may look different from this widow's world, but she teaches us three critical lessons on hope.

1. There is no hopelessness in God.

Our circumstances never tell the whole story; they tell only what we can see. But the eternal God is our refuge, and always, always underneath are his everlasting arms. You may be facing big unknowns. You may be at the end of your own ability, and you may not see the way through your circumstances. But the end of your rope is the middle of God's story.

First Kings 17 tells us God initially provided for Elijah through ravens, who made a daily bread delivery to him. If that seems crazy, it's just as farfetched that God provided for Elijah through a woman—and not only a woman, but a widow, and a gentile at that!

The end of your rope is the middle of God's story.

As a gentile widow living outside of Israel, she was outside the protections of Jewish law and would have been among the most poor and needy. But God's resources are unlimited and his timing is perfect. We may not see a way through, but there is never hopelessness with God.

2. There is no lack in God.

I imagine this young mom watched her flour and oil dwindle for months. Maybe if she knocked every last bit from the container's sides and left her oil jar to hang upside down, she'd get just enough to make one last loaf.

Long before she ever reached the place of need, God knew how he would meet it.

Her flour was getting low, but God would send Elijah.

Her oil was running thin, but God would send Elijah.

She began to gather sticks for a last meal, but God would send Elijah.

Right now, in your desperate need, God knows how he's going to care for you. In fact, God knows how he will meet needs you don't even have yet.

God will provide guidance as you need it.

God will provide wisdom as you need it.

God will provide comfort as you need it.

God will provide materially as you need it.
God will provide grace as you need it.
God will provide for each circumstance as you need it.

3. There is no lack in God—but there are tests of faith.

God owns the cattle on a thousand hills, and he could have hand-delivered one to this woman. But instead, he asked her to trust and obey. She had to give the last of what she had to Elijah, trusting God's promise that he wouldn't let her flour or oil run out until the drought was over.

See, God wanted more than to simply meet this woman's needs. It wasn't just that she was physically poor; she was spiritually impoverished as well.

God wanted this woman living in a gentile country outside of Israel to know him as the one true God. He was wooing her.

When she trusted God with everything she had, God provided everything she needed.

And of course, God was faithful to his promise as he only can be. For three years, every time she reached into that jar of flour, there was enough. Every time she poured oil from the jar, there was enough. Every time she made cakes for Elijah, there was enough. When her growing boy was hungry, there was enough.

God provided for Elijah, this woman, and her son when she trusted God with everything she had.

God wants the same for us. When you find yourself at the end of hope and in deep need, God will meet your need—he promises us that. But he wants more for you. He wants to feed your soul and give you eternal hope beyond this life.

Our tests don't show up in empty oil jars. They're more likely to show up in our bank account, a health scare, a teetering marriage, or a parenting struggle.

Before Dan's death, as a young mom of four children under five, I faced a test of faith in our finances. It was mid-December, I'd just resigned as a part-time attorney to stay home, and Dan and I had taken a leap of faith to start tithing from the little we had. We were pinching every penny we could find when Dan's employer retroactively moved several of his big accounts to another store, canceling the final-quarter bonus he'd been accruing all year. There went our money for Christmas and the holiday food we'd need for our extended family's visit. We were broke.

A couple mornings later, Dan and I got into a tense argument. I was pushing back against this whole retroactive accounting, but Dan couldn't do anything about it. Frustrated and angry, I got in my minivan for errands and, backing down the long driveway, swung over to our mailbox. I was leafing through mostly bills when an envelope caught my attention. It was from Publix and inside were five $100 gift certificates. *Five hundred dollars.* Months earlier, I'd dropped my name into a cardboard box while grocery shopping and had thought no more of it.

I zipped back up the driveway and went inside the house to show Dan. As it turned out, I was able to buy a pack of gum with the gift certificates and get the change in cash. We had Christmas presents under the tree and food for visiting family after all. We had trusted God with our little. That trust had been tested, but there was never any lack with God.

There is no hopelessness in God. And while there are tests of faith, there is no lack in God either. The same God who provided for Elijah and this widow in drought and desperation is the same God who is faithful to us as well, if we will trust and obey.

Biblical Hope Is More than a Birthday Wish

Let's define what we mean by *hope*, because we sprinkle this word around like confetti in our everyday conversations. Sometimes we use *hope* to mean optimism or wishful thinking: "I hope this car makes it," "I hope it doesn't rain this weekend," or "I hope I get that job I applied for." Optimism is the glass-half-full attitude that looks on the bright side and sees a favorable future. Like a birthday wish, it longs for something good to happen. I'm all for optimism, but biblical hope is more than happy thoughts that things will turn out well.

Optimism and wishful thinking are based on possibilities while the hope we have in God is a certainty. I love Pam Tebow's definition of hope as the "dynamic confidence that God will come through."[1]

Optimism and wishful thinking aren't enough when life is too hard to handle and we've exhausted every resource we know. When we're staring at the frayed ends of the rope of our own possibility, we need to know our hope is anchored in an unchangeable God who can only ever be faithful. Our hope is anchored in the God of hope.[2]

Our hope in God is certain because it isn't rooted in something but in Someone. No matter what we're facing, no matter what our circumstances, no matter how impossible it feels, we have hope because God is sovereign over our circumstances.

In fact, it's only when circumstances seem impossible that we need hope. Who needs hope when you can see your way through and you have the ability to make something happen? Hope only matters when we arrive at the end of our rope.

G. K. Chesterton writes, "Hope means hoping when things are hopeless, or it is no virtue at all. . . . As long as matters are really hopeful, hope is mere flattery or platitude; it is only when everything is hopeless that hope begins to be a strength."[3]

When I look at people in the Bible who are anchored into this kind of hope, Abraham is one who stands out. We first meet Abraham (then called Abram) in Genesis 11 at the ripe age of seventy. He's married to Sarah (then called Sarai), and the one distinctive description given is they are childless because Sarah is unable to conceive. I imagine the decades of disappointment Abraham and Sarah had already endured. Yet five years later, God makes a startling promise to Abraham: Leave your country, your home, and your family, and follow me, because I will make a great nation from you.[4]

A nation from Abraham? He was seventy-five years old, and Sarah was sixty-five! Without questioning, Abraham did as the Lord had told him and set out with Sarah and their household to follow God. When they arrived in Canaan, God appeared to Abraham, confirming his promise: "To your offspring I will give this land" (Genesis 12:7). Abraham built an altar at this place of renewed promise and worshiped God.

God moved mightily in Abraham's life over the years. He was faithful through drought, through Abraham's misdoing in Egypt, through division of the land with his nephew Lot, and through warfare with five kings.

Still, as the years ticked by, month after heart-wrenching month, Sarah remained barren.

When Abraham grieved that his servant would inherit everything, God renewed his promise, telling Abraham to "look up at the sky and count the stars—if indeed you can count them. . . . So shall your offspring be" (Genesis 15:5).

At this point, Abraham and Sarah took matters into their own hands. God had promised; shouldn't they make it happen?

Defaulting to cultural norms, Abraham fathered a child through Sarah's servant, Hagar, who gave birth to Ishmael.

But God never intended to fulfill his promise to Abraham through Ishmael. Thirteen years later, he told Abraham that Sarah would have a son.[5] Sarah? She was well past any natural ability to conceive.

Sure enough, when Abraham was one hundred years old and Sarah was ninety, she gave birth to Isaac. Through Isaac's miraculous birth, God fulfilled his promise to make Abraham into a great nation (the Israelites), through whom God would bring his Son Jesus.

The New Testament writer of Romans writes about Abraham's hope:

> ***Against all hope***, Abraham in hope believed and so became the father of many nations, just as it had been said to him, "So shall your offspring be." Without weakening in his faith, he faced the fact that his body was ***as good as dead***—since he was about a hundred years old—and that Sarah's womb ***was also dead***. Yet he did not waver through unbelief regarding the promise of God, but was strengthened in his faith and gave glory to God, ***being fully persuaded that God had power to do what he had promised.***
>
> Romans 4:18–21, emphasis added

What God promises, God will bring about. His timeline may be much, *much* longer than ours, and his ways different from anything we could imagine. But hope in God means God will fulfill his promises, in his way and in his timing.

Hope fills the gap between God's promise and God's fulfillment of that promise.

We cannot place our hope on how the promise will be fulfilled.

We cannot place our hope on when the promise will be fulfilled.

We can only place our hope on WHO will fulfill the promise.

Need to Borrow Hope?

Sometimes it's hardest to hope when we've hoped for so long. Abraham waited twenty-five years for the fulfillment of God's promise. God's *perfect plan* meant waiting two and a half decades. Not one day of that wait had God forgotten. Not one day was wasted.

When we get exhausted and when possibilities are dashed over and over again, our hope can become threadbare. It's in these moments we need to borrow hope.

Lindsey Wheeler writes in her book *Sacred Tears* about a poignant moment when a friend showed up to deliver hope. For more than twelve years, Lindsey has dealt with the chronic effects of Lyme disease as well as the challenges of raising her special-needs daughter. Most days, she says, are spent in bed or on a couch battling debilitating pain.

Hope fills the gap between God's promise and God's fulfillment of that promise.

Lindsey writes that in an especially dark time, her friend Jenn sent Lindsey several messages that Lindsey didn't respond to. Knowing this was unlike Lindsey, and knowing she must really be struggling, Jenn and her husband drove cross-country for a visit. Lindsey writes:

> Chris and I sat across the table from our dear friends, and I told them I had simply lost hope. I described the heavy pain we were feeling and how impossible it all felt. I told them that my faith was just barely hanging on.

> Gifted with discernment, my friend said, "We know you don't have hope, so let us hope for you."[6]

No pep talk. No Scriptures. Simply the presence of a friend who offered to lend hope.

I remember having to borrow hope at one point when my own was flagging. One morning after Dan died, I was mentally, emotionally, physically, and spiritually spent. Hanging on by a thread, I reached out to a friend.

"I need prayer" was all I could text.

A few minutes later, my phone lit up with a reply. My friend happened to be gathered with other families in a friend's home that morning.

"Everyone stopped and prayed," she texted back, and she sent a picture of moms and kids of all ages on couches, on chairs, and on the floor, all with heads bowed in prayer.

I borrowed their hope that day.

Even if you don't have a community you can turn to when your hope is wearing thin, borrow my hope today. With everything in me, I assure you that God will never abandon you. While our walks may be different, I have been in the thin place, and I can tell you, hope in God will never disappoint you. Reach out and take hold of the dynamic hope that God will come through for you in this.

> And not only this, but we also celebrate in our tribulations, knowing that tribulation brings about perseverance; and perseverance, proven character; and proven character, hope; **and hope does not disappoint, because the love of God has been poured out within our hearts through the Holy Spirit who was given to us.**
>
> Romans 5:3–5 NASB, emphasis added

Have You Misplaced Hope?

Sometimes we transfer our hope to something or someone without realizing it, until our hope is gone.

When Dan died suddenly, I realized I had some big holes in my theology. Somewhere along the way, I'd taken on assumptions, giving them the polish of godliness, and parked some of my hope there. One of those came about when we decided to trust God with the size of our family. I never set out to have a large family. I wanted three kids, Dan wanted two, and it was a huge leap of faith outside of my own upbringing and my own logical reasoning to give God full say-so over how many children we had.

Three children squared with our plans. Having a fourth child and then fifth weren't expected, but they were more than welcome. We put measures in place, and for a while, I thought we'd always have five children. Out of the blue, God began to work on my heart, and after months of wrestling, Dan and I surrendered our plans for whatever family God had for us.

To my delight, I got pregnant two more times, and both times, I held my breath and trusted God. We knew the risks of having children in my late thirties and early forties were higher, but we'd signed up for those risks. But I never dreamed God would give us children and then not let Dan live to see them raised. My expectation was that if we stepped out with big faith to trust God with our family size, he would give us a long life together to see them raised. Fair deal, right?

But I'd misplaced my hope. God had never made that promise in Scripture.

We so easily build our hopes on illusory expectations and buy in to false promises that can't deliver. If your hope is flagging right now, it could be because you've parked it with someone or something other than God.

Let's look at the differences between misplaced hope and God-given hope.

Misplaced Hope	*God-Given Hope*
If I eat right and exercise, I will avoid all health issues.	I can steward my body well, but all my days have been ordained by God.
I will be happy when __________ happens.	I choose joy now because only God can satisfy my heart's longings.
If I do all the right things, my life will go as planned.	If I follow God, I can trust his plans.
Following God in this big step of faith means he will make the way easy.	Following God means he will equip and sustain me even if the path is difficult.
If I take my children to church and teach them about God, they'll have deep faith as adults.	I'm responsible to love God, teach my children, and entrust them to God.
If my actions are godly, I will be treated fairly.	If my actions are godly, I can trust God with all outcomes.

Ultimately for the believer, our hope leads us beyond our circumstances here to an eternity with God, without pain, sickness, suffering, or death.

Though we can pray for physical healing, our hope is not healing. *It is Christ*. Everyone healed will suffer something else that will eventually end in death.

Though we can pray for a better marriage or to be married, our hope is not a person. *It is Christ.* No person, no matter how loving, can ever satisfy us.

Though we can pray for a better job or a business turnaround, our hope is not in finances. *It is in Christ.* No position or amount of money can satisfy us.

Our hope is found only in Christ. And when life strips away things or people or positions we thought would always be there, we're in a good place to develop complete satisfaction in Christ alone.

A Prayer for Hope

Heavenly Father, I am weary and my hope has worn thin. Help me know in my bones that hope in you never disappoints. Keep me from going before you or taking matters into my own hands. Help me wait well, with assurance that you always bring about what you have promised and that waiting on your perfect timing is always worth it. Show me where I have misplaced my hope and help me be fully satisfied in you alone. Refresh me today because my hope is in you, my God of hope. In Jesus' name, amen.

11

Let's Be Awkward Together

> Let each of you look not only to his own interests, but also to the interests of others.
>
> Philippians 2:4 ESV

> What does love look like? It has the hands to help others. It has the feet to hasten to the poor and needy. It has eyes to see misery and want. It has the ears to hear the sighs and sorrows of men. That is what love looks like.
>
> Augustine

How's your list coming?" my friend Rhonda asked. I grimaced silently, trying to move past her question because, truth was, I hadn't made a list. Weeks before, she'd asked me to keep a running list of things that needed to be fixed around my house. She planned to bring a group out one Saturday to tackle the list. Goodness knows, I had a slew of things I needed help with.

But I hadn't been able to bring myself to put anything on the list. I knew my friend's heart and her sincere desire to give us practical help. She'd already shown up once, keeping her eyes peeled for what needed to be done and then quietly going about doing it. Now she was asking for my input. But each time I thought of a task, it either felt too big to ask someone to do it or small enough that we should have been able to handle it.

For example, our suburban lot was filled with huge granddaddy oak trees—it's one of the reasons we'd bought the house in the first place. But some of the branches were now arching over the shed and back porch, and several smaller oaks needed to be taken down. One oak had overgrown vines that ran up the trunk and branches and had wound their way onto the eaves of our house. These oaks sure needed attention, but asking friends to help with this seemed too big of an ask.

There were smaller jobs, like fencing that needed to be put up on one side of the house, and the spring leaf litter to rake up. But I had seven kids. We were healthy and able. If I put something like that on the list, I worried friends would think we were asking them to pick up our slack.

Worried that tasks were either too big or too small, I never made the list. Looking back now, my excuses seem ridiculous. Yes, my children were capable, but they were also navigating deep trauma, and I was overwhelmed trying to hold everything together by myself. I would have happily helped another person with the very tasks I couldn't bring myself to put on the list.

So I pressed on, the kids and I doing what we could while the yard continued to get worse. I wish I had given myself permission not to expect so much of myself and to take the help offered. Not only did I miss out on practical help we could have used, but I robbed my friends of the gift they wanted to give us.

For the record, I did accept a lot of help. People brought meals for months, asked our family to join theirs for holidays, fixed a water heater, replaced that water heater, came Christmas caroling with hot chocolate and loaded stockings for the kids, cleaned the house, mowed the lawn, sent gift cards, showed up to listen, prayed for us with countless prayers, coached my boys, sponsored church camp, cleaned up after a hurricane, sent notes and texts, gave us a car, and did many other things without fanfare that only heaven will one day reveal.

We would not be where we are without that help.

But I turned away help as well, and didn't ask for help when I sorely needed it. From conversations with friends, I know I'm not alone. Why is asking for help so hard?

Learning to receive doesn't come naturally to most of us. Even when we're feeling overwhelmed up to our neck, our default is to fake that everything is fine and keep up a façade that we've got it all together. That we've got everything under control. Asking for help makes us feel inept, vulnerable, and awkward.

I never made that list for my friend because I was too scared for anyone to see my incapability. Sharing my need felt like exposing all the places where I wasn't enough—enough of a housekeeper or bookkeeper or organizer or hard worker. It meant letting go of the me I put on social media and presented on Sunday mornings, and instead letting people see my life as it really was.

Learning to ask for help means letting go of the façade that we've got it all together.

But it wasn't just vulnerability keeping me stuck. It was pride. Pride I hadn't realized was there.

Asking for help is as much about chiseling the pride from our heart as meeting our need.

Learning to ask for help means letting go of the façade that we've got it all together. It means cleaning out the plaque of pride gunking up our hearts and keeping us from admitting we need help. It means inviting others into our lack and watching God use them to meet our need.

It Takes Cheerful Givers and Gracious Receivers

Most of us are happy to be the one giving help. How many times have you delivered the casserole, sent the gift card, or shown up to help? It feels good to be the one giving. Giving often means sacrificing our own time, and it brings warm joy to drop a hot meal off with a sick friend, scrub floors for ministry day, or donate to a GoFundMe when someone's facing an unexpected difficulty.

If you've been in the church for any number of years, you've probably heard multiple sermons on giving. We know as believers that we're called to give. Whole books have been written (and ministries formed) on teaching us how to give well. I mean, God loves a cheerful giver, right?

But for someone to give, there must be someone to receive. When have you heard a sermon on learning to receive? In all my years, I've never heard it preached. Yet receiving well has as much a place in the body of Christ as giving well.

My friend Eleana found herself in a crash course of learning to receive. She's got a generous heart and has always been there with meals for neighbors and friends in her Sunday school class. As a young mom with a kindergartner and toddler in tow, she began experiencing symptoms that sent her to the doctor. After a round of tests, she was diagnosed with cancer, and the prognosis felt like a gut punch. She immediately began chemotherapy, which made her too weak to care for her family.

"I was flat on my back and didn't have a choice. I had to let people come into my house to help," Eleana recalled. "We were in the fight of our life. My husband was doing all he could to stay on top of the medical bills, his work, and the kids, and I was so sick I could barely lift my head."

She says God knew her most intimate needs, and "he sent in the troops." Women brought meals every night for six weeks as she endured grueling chemo. Her sister-in-law came every Friday to clean, never asking but simply showing up so Eleana could come back from chemo to a clean home. Her mother-in-law stepped in to homeschool her children each day, and one day, another friend showed up to throw Eleana's two-year-old a birthday party. Eleana said that only God knew how big birthday parties were to their family and what having that celebration in the midst of their pain meant. The bonds created with those who stepped in to help during her cancer treatment forged deep friendships.

"We have such a connection. I would have missed out on that and those friendships had I not allowed them to come in and help," Eleana told me.

It feels awkward to ask for help. I know it's hard to let go of pride and let others see that everything actually isn't under control, but we weren't made to walk through seasons of deep pain alone. We could love each other so much better and so much more honestly if we just agreed to be awkward together.

As the body of Christ, we need to be both generous givers and gracious receivers. As I let God chisel the pride keeping me from making that list, I began to see why learning to receive is vital for our Christian walk. Let me show you six reasons why.

1. Receiving builds up the body of Christ.

As Christians, we're called to live together as a community of believers. Community isn't walking through the same hallways on Sunday. Community happens when we love each other, share together, are honest and vulnerable with each other, give generously to each other, and receive graciously from each other.

Deep bonds aren't formed just because we hold the same theological beliefs, but as we do life together through those beliefs. God knits us together as we serve one another, look to each other's interests, and carry each other's burdens. When we give, share, serve, receive, see need, meet need, and accept help over and over, we weave separate individuals into a flourishing and committed community.

The body of Christ is built through givers and receivers—those generously showing love through a mailed card, a hot meal, or a mowed lawn, and those graciously receiving love through vulnerability and an open, humble heart. We need both parties; we're never just one or the other. God didn't create some as givers and others as receivers. We move back and forth from one to the other. In any given day, I might lend a listening ear and mom wisdom to one friend while getting help from another who's shuffling my child home from practice. In different seasons, we may find ourselves needing to ask for help and depending on help to make it through, but then, as we find our footing once again, we offer help to someone else.

2. Receiving cultivates our own compassion.

I realized this one evening in a conversation with my oldest son. He was in college when his dad died, and one night, he called me with a quandary. A couple who were dear family friends had offered to buy him his college textbooks for the semester.

"Should I let them do this, Mom?" I remember him being a bit choked up over their kindness, but also conflicted.

"Ben, they want to because they love you," I said. "I want you to think about this: You're headed to medical school. You'll be at a place one day where you'll be the one giving medical care on a mission trip or maybe in your own practice. In order to understand that patient, you need to know what it feels like to receive so that you can give well."

Those words brought clarity to my own conflicted feelings even as I spoke them.

Another friend told me that cultivating empathy through the practice of receiving has become a core principle at a food bank she helps run. At the beginning of the year, each volunteer who helps distribute food goes home with a box of food, regardless of need, so they understand what it feels like to receive food help. Operating with compassion helps us see that pride has no place in either receiving help or giving it.

3. Receiving allows God to answer our prayers.

On one hand, we beg God to meet our need, and then in self-sufficient pride, we hamstring the very provision we've prayed for. God promises to meet our need, and he can certainly do that any way he wants. But often, God answers our prayers for help through the hands and feet of others.

Remember Eleana? Years after beating cancer, she found herself walking through another difficult season when her husband unexpectedly lost his job. It was a devastating time and they were deeply hurt by the circumstances. They had been a one-income family, already on a razor-thin budget without any extras to cut. After months of unemployment, Eleana walked into her garage one day to get meat from their deep freezer for dinner, only to find there was none left.

"I was so scared and so angry," Eleana recalls. Alone in the garage, she said she began yelling out loud at the whole situation.

"Thirty minutes later, my husband called me out to the garage and opened up the freezer. It was packed full of meat. Not only meat, but organic meat! We'd never been able to afford organic meat."

A friend had backed his truck into the driveway and filled their entire freezer. As Eleana told me this story, she added, "When [God] is faithful and he does things, I get giddy because he is over the top. There's no denying that it's from the Lord."

4. Receiving completes the obedience of others.

When we receive help, it's often because God has nudged someone else to give. A few weeks after my husband died, I opened my mailbox to find a check from another widow. She was an older woman in my church who was disabled and helping to raise her grandson. I was so moved that she had sent this unsolicited check, and stared at it with a mix of awe and grateful humility. But how could I cash it when I knew she had needs of her own? So I set it aside, unable to bring myself to cash it.

But God kept working on my heart and teaching me what it meant to receive well. This widow had generously given, and I needed to graciously receive. Was I going to refuse her gift? Maybe she *had* given sacrificially, but wouldn't God take care of her? She had already impacted me by showing me what it looked like to give from your own need. And so with deep gratitude, I honored her gift and deposited the check into our account.

To refuse someone's offer to help is to deny others the blessing of giving help.

When we humble ourselves to graciously receive, we complete the obedience of others following God's nudge to give that help.

When we humble ourselves to graciously receive, we complete the obedience of others following God's nudge to give that help.

5. Receiving develops our humility.

God is not asking us to be *humiliated*. That should never be part of giving or receiving. But God does want us to have *humility*. Humiliation is about shame and embarrassment; humility is open and soft-hearted. Godly humility says, "I'm not too hung up on myself or my perception to receive your gift of love," and, "Thank you for walking with me practically through this need."

My friend and fellow podcaster Jenn, who helps run the food pantry I mentioned earlier, is used to being in positions of responsibility. She told me she doesn't often ask for help because she doesn't want people to lose confidence in her or think she's unorganized. "I'm a very resourceful and capable person, and I'm usually the one helping other people," Jenn said. But in the midst of a surprise adoption, she saw the blessing of asking for help.

Jenn and her husband had three teens and zero plans to foster or adopt more children when they learned of a baby and a toddler needing a home. They offered a tentative yes, knowing so much had to fall into place, that placement was a long shot. But by week's end, that long shot became reality, and they had three days to prepare their home and life for a baby and toddler.

"I was stress-paralyzed," Jenn recalls. "I was sitting there thinking, *We're adding children to our family and I don't know what to do*."

She texted her friend Rachel, who immediately texted back: "Sit tight. We're on our way."

Rachel and another friend came over with toys, clothes, and all kinds of things the kids would need.

"They took over," Jenn said. Her friends reorganized kitchen cupboards, rearranged her family room, and set up bedrooms to get her home completely ready to welcome her two new children.

Instead of the humiliation she'd feared, Jenn's humility brought blessing for her and her friends.

"It was one of the more poignant moments during that adoption where God used them to love us well," Jenn recalled. "If we hadn't asked for help, we would have missed out on that."

6. Receiving makes us like Christ.

Here we come to my favorite reason to receive well. We often talk about how Jesus was a generous giver. He gave his life for us by dying on the cross for our sins, giving us eternal life with him. Jesus gives us peace with God and the peace of God. He gives us access to the Father and abundant life on this side of heaven.

But Christ was also a gracious receiver. Jesus received regular financial support from a group of women who traveled with him and the disciples.

> Jesus traveled about from one town and village to another, proclaiming the good news of the kingdom of God. The Twelve were with him, and also some women who had been cured of evil spirits and diseases: Mary (called Magdalene) from whom seven demons had come out; Joanna the wife of Chuza, the manager of Herod's household; Susanna; and many others. **These women were helping to support them out of their own means.**
>
> Luke 8:1–3, emphasis added

Jesus graciously received throughout his ministry. When he fed the five thousand, it was after he received fish and loaves from a boy in the crowd. As Jesus traveled throughout Israel, he received regular hospitality. With no home of his own, Scripture tells us Jesus stayed with Peter's mother-in-law and the sibling trio of Mary, Martha, and Lazarus. He also ate grain from others' fields as he traveled, a practice where farmers intentionally left some of their grain for the poor. And when Jesus sent the seventy-two disciples to minister throughout Galilee, he instructed them to rely completely on the gifts of others. They weren't to take any money with them but to receive whatever food their hosts offered.

God could have provided for Jesus any number of ways during his earthly ministry. He chose to care for the King of kings through the continued support, gifts, and hospitality of others.

Being a gracious receiver is just as Christlike as being a generous giver.

Getting Over Awkward in Giving

Okay, so maybe you're convinced we should be both givers *and receivers* as part of the body of Christ. But learning to receive isn't the only awkward part. Figuring out when and how to best help someone can be awkward too.

Have you ever wanted to help someone but you weren't sure how? Have you ever worried you might be intruding if you offered help? Or thought they might not need the kind of help you want to give? Maybe, like me, you've seen that the need is so great it paralyzes you from doing anything at all.

I want to share two guidelines I've learned from others that have helped me get over the awkwardness when I'm giving help.

First, when the need seems overwhelming and you're paralyzed from offering help, remember this: Just because you can't do everything doesn't mean you shouldn't do something. When

Crystal Paine of moneysavingmom.com shared this on her Instagram, it really hit home.

None of us can do everything. But when a family member, friend, or acquaintance is going through a difficult time, we can all do something. And everything adds up. Never let the size of the need keep you from offering the thing you can do.

Just because you can't do everything doesn't mean you shouldn't do something.

Second (and my friend Rhonda—the one who asked me to make the list—taught me this), when someone is going through a difficult time, expect God to reveal need and then follow his nudge.

Ask God for spiritual sensitivity to see need around you, and then, when God shows you that need, trust his nudge instead of second-guessing it. Rhonda is legendary for this in my community (though she would never say it). She even taught her children to look for need and to follow God's nudge. This has led her and her family to do things like distribute Chick-fil-A biscuits to a roomful of patients getting chemotherapy when her son began receiving weekly treatments, and order basketball shoes for two brothers when she saw they were the only ones playing without the team shoes.

Friend, I know in this season of difficulty, it's vulnerable to open up and let others help. To make it easier, I'd encourage you to make two lists.

On the first list, write down tasks you need help with, like yardwork, meals, errands, or small home repairs. Pray over this list, asking God to bring others to meet these needs and to prepare your heart to share when they come. Some people in your life will give the general "Call me when you need something," and you'll sense they aren't ready to commit to helping. But others really want to know how to help, and you can share a need from this list.

Second, make a list of prayer needs. When someone asks how they can pray for you, share a specific need. When people asked me, I gave them the name of one of my kids or a task that was overwhelming me. It was reassuring to know people were covering our specific needs and struggles in prayer.

And while you may be mostly receiving now, you will find your footing again. You'll be in a place again to give with the compassion God is cultivating in you right now. And when that time comes, remember you don't have to do everything to do something. Look for need and then follow God's nudge.

A Prayer to Give and Receive

Lord, you know my needs and you have the perfect provisions for that. Help me root out my pride and learn to receive from others that I might be part of building up the body of Christ. Grow my compassion and empathy as others help me so I can turn around and see others' needs and be a generous giver. In all things and in all ways, make me like Christ. In Jesus' holy name, amen.

12

Let God Reshape Your Shattered Heart

Those who sow with tears will reap with songs of joy. Those who go out weeping, carrying seed to sow, will return with songs of joy, carrying sheaves with them.

Psalm 126:5–6

The deepest things I have learned in my own life have come from the deepest suffering. And out of the deepest waters and the hottest fires have come the deepest things I know about God.

Elisabeth Elliot

They say what doesn't kill you makes you stronger, but that's not the whole truth.

Because what doesn't kill you can make you bitter. What doesn't kill you can leave you moving through life with your heart numb. And what doesn't kill you can lead you to make bad decisions with even worse consequences.

Circumstances alone cannot make us stronger. It's the choices we make in our circumstances that allow God to reshape us and leave us more like Christ than before.

"I just want to fast-forward through this," I groaned to my friend Gina over our phone call. I was a couple months into our new not-so-normal, and the inner work of letting go of the life I wanted and taking steps forward was grueling. "I know God will be faithful, but I just want to be fifteen years out and be able to look back to see it."

There was a quiet pause on the other end of the line, and then she spoke words that hit their mark: "Yes, but you won't be who God wants you to be unless you walk through it."

Oh, how we want to get past the pain and scary unknown so we can feel good again. Taking steps forward when life has imploded can feel like walking through wet cement. What might look like a tiny, easy step to someone else takes summoning up deep courage and strength for us. Things that should be easy feel way too difficult.

I remember thinking I needed to tape a sign to the back of my bedroom door before heading out each morning that said **You can do hard things.** Because everything felt hard. Every day I was facing another new task. Another unknown outcome. Another unwanted step. In shattering disappointment, we long for life to be back to normal, to once again have mornings when we wake up excited for what the day holds with the energy to fully meet it.

It's not so much that we doubt God will restore that kind of excitement to us; it's that we dread the excruciating walk to get there. If only we could bypass the painful valley and fast-forward to the mountaintop. . . .

But my friend Gina was right. There are lessons we can only learn, good we will only see, truths we will only come to know personally as we walk *through* the hard place.

Here's what I know to be true about lessons in the hard place: When we trust God with the broken pieces of our life, God can reshape what's shattered.

Melissa discovered this when her marriage fell apart and her husband asked for a divorce. She had stepped away from her career years earlier to stay home with their three little girls and loved watching them flourish in their dance and music classes. Her marriage wasn't perfect, but it felt stable and she was content. When her husband first hinted at problems in their marriage and that he was unhappy, she easily convinced him to go with her to counseling. Thinking this was the answer to getting their marriage back on track, she was blindsided when her husband announced one evening he wanted a divorce.

When we trust God with the broken pieces of our life, God can reshape what's shattered.

A volley of words followed, and for the first time she realized how unhappy her husband had been and how intent he was on divorce. It was a word she could barely utter—a word that belonged to other families. She became desperate, saying things she thought might rescue her marriage. She told her husband she'd do whatever he needed, begged him to stay. But her words and tears had no effect, and with Melissa wondering how her life had unraveled so fast, she heard his final words: *I've never loved you.*

Over the next months, nearly every part of Melissa's life either disappeared or drastically changed. While she had once spent long days with her girls, she now spent two weekends a month packing their suitcases, dropping them with her soon-to-be-ex-husband, and going home to a pin-drop quiet house. She was emotionally devastated and financially strapped. A fog of grief descended over her, and she was thrust into a world of haggling over assets and bills, and communicating through lawyers with the man she would still love, honor, and cherish if he would just change his mind. The finality of divorce brought a new level of despair, as she faced a future she never saw coming and surely didn't want. She couldn't imagine how her heart would survive such pain.

But God did much more than help Melissa survive. He reshaped her broken heart altogether. Her once highly structured personality softened as she focused on her girls and the time she had with them. Forced to let go of the perfect life she'd dreamed of, she discovered what really mattered and what didn't. As she figured out shared custody and single parenting and her new part-time work, her faith deepened. The storm that threatened to wreck her only made her anchor more deeply in God and his Word.

Several months after her divorce became final, Melissa spoke up during the prayer and praise time of her Bible study. She acknowledged through tears that while she would never wish to go through what she'd endured, she would never want to go back to the person she was before it happened. God had forever reshaped her.

The Refiner's Work

Like Melissa, most of us would never volunteer for the kind of difficulty that completely upends our world. But our goal in life as Christ followers isn't to make it to old age dodging as much difficulty as possible. Our goal is to become like Christ. And one of the chief ways God makes us like Jesus is through suffering.

When circumstances break our heart, we're in a good place for God to go ahead and clean it out.

"As long as I'm broken open, Lord, you might as well clean me out," became one of my new prayers in my own suffering.

When circumstances break our heart, we're in a good place for God to go ahead and clean it out.

Suffering often reveals the idols we've been clinging to. It brings to the surface sin we may not even be aware we've tolerated. Sins like selfishness, envy, entitlement, anger, unforgiveness, judgment, legalism, envy, impatience, and more.

Our suffering isn't always the consequence of a specific sin we've committed. That can happen, but we also suffer because we live in a fallen world—a world of disease and car accidents and bodies that are perishing. As believers, we don't get a free pass from suffering, but God will never waste it. "Suffering is never for nothing," said Elisabeth Elliot.[1]

As long as we're here, in this place of shattering loss, let's allow God to use it to make us like Christ, like the refiner who uses the fire to remove impurities from his cherished gold and make it shine.

"In all this you greatly rejoice, though now for a little while you may have had to suffer grief in all kinds of trials. These have come so that the proven genuineness of your faith—of greater worth than gold, which perishes even though refined by fire—may result in praise, glory and honor when Jesus Christ is revealed" (1 Peter 1:6–7).

The refiner's fire, painful though it is, produces in us character far more valuable than any earthly treasure. If I were to hold out a rough rock with veins of gold running through it in one hand, and a gleaming, polished gold nugget in the other, which would you choose? Every one of us would immediately see the value, usefulness, and beauty of the purified gold.

As we walk through suffering, we too are being refined. Our Refiner sees both the impurity in us that needs to be removed and the beauty that will come forth.

The ancients used fire to purify gold. The refiner first prepared the fire to reach temperatures over 1800° Fahrenheit, and then placed the gold ore in a clay crucible over the fire. With great care and constant attention, the refiner would stir the gold until it melted, and the dross—impurities in the gold without value—would rise to the top. He would skim off the dross and discard it. Over and over again, the refiner would stir the melted gold in the crucible over the fire, skimming off the dross and increasing the value and purity of the gold.

And the result of the refining process? Author Kay Arthur explains the process: "He has taken what was dull and made it beautiful. Potential value has become actual value. And the fire—the guarded, guided, relentless fire—made the difference. The fire allowed ordinary ore from the earth to be transformed into treasure."[2]

You may feel the flames of the fire licking you right now. But the fires God allows are never meant to destroy you; they are meant to refine you. The fire of suffering brings our impurities to the surface like little else in life, and—if we yield our hearts to God—God can remove them, creating eternal beauty in us that reflects his glory.

Good Lessons in Hard Places

Tucked inside unexpected hard is unexpected good. Though you and I would not have chosen this suffering, we have an opportunity to see God in ways we never would have otherwise, to find God faithful in our helpless dependence on him, to chisel out idols we've clung to in misplaced hope, to discover that God's promises hold up in the worst circumstances, and to fall in love with God all over again as he walks us through the hard place.

Tucked inside unexpected hard is unexpected good.

Suffering seems to make these lessons come faster and more clearly than other times in life, and our brokenness often makes us a captive audience, tills our heart, and spiritually awakens us so that we're ripe to learn.

You can't go back to the girl you were before this all happened. And if we let God do his deep work in us, we won't want to go back to the girl we were before.

What are some of the lessons we're ripe to learn in suffering?

Suffering teaches us what the good life really is. The point of this life is not what God will do for us or how he will meet our expectations and the entitlements we hold. The point of this life is how we can spend it for God.

Suffering teaches us about real joy. Looking at the shattered pieces of life as we wanted it, we can wonder if we'll ever experience joy again. Maybe it will happen months down the road when we've been able to move through the shock and hard emotions. Or maybe, if God brings that one thing we've been praying for, we'll feel joy again.

The surprise is that joy comes not after the hard, but right in the midst of it. God gives us pockets of joy while we're still processing sorrow. Those pockets of joy are like a deep hug in the hard place. They're assurance that—like the refiner who carefully tends his melted treasure—God has not abandoned us or our future.

When Paul wrote his letter to the Philippian church, urging them to rejoice in all things, he was in prison. Paul had been arrested while preaching and was sent from one prison to another until he finally reached Rome. Paul could easily have seen his time in prisons waiting for appeal as wasted suffering, taking him away from his work as a church planter. Instead, Paul found joy in the midst of suffering. "Rejoice in the Lord always. I will say it again: Rejoice!" (Philippians 4:4).

Suffering teaches us about real peace. I have to admit, I'm a girl who loves some peace and quiet. Put me in a hammock on a deck overlooking the Smoky Mountains and I can exhale every bit of stress. I'd also take writing in my bedroom when the kitchen's clean, my kids are quietly engaged in worthwhile activities, and the Crock-Pot is simmering with dinner. But that's not peace; *that's calm.*

Peace isn't the absence of difficulty;
peace is the presence of God.

God's presence ushers in his supernatural peace, which holds us steady when life shifts around us. God's peace doesn't ignore the pain, the tumult of emotions, or the upheaval of change that suffering can bring. But God's peace allows us to say it is well with our soul when all is not right with our circumstances.

While in prison, Paul also wrote to the Philippians, "Do not be anxious about anything, but in every situation, by prayer and petition, with thanksgiving, present your requests to God. And the peace of God, which transcends all understanding, will guard your hearts and your minds in Christ Jesus" (Philippians 4:6–7).

Suffering teaches us about real treasure. I have another admission, and this one hurts to write openly: For years, I pined away for a bigger house. There were nine of us in a three-ish-bedroom house that we'd originally bought to live in for a year.

It was not the house I meant to raise my kids in. But then, the housing bubble popped, the economy tanked, and we ended up staying in that house for fourteen years. My frustration with everything that house wasn't revealed ugly heart issues I needed to work on. My prayers sounded more like complaints. But pray and complain I did, thinking life would be good if only I had a bigger, better, newer house.

Then Dan died. That day, our house overflowed with family, neighbors, church friends, and Dan's bosses who came to be with us. The upstairs air conditioner had broken the night before, and the downstairs unit froze when it couldn't keep up with such a packed space in Florida's June heat. The dishes weren't done, our beds were unmade, and my paper stacks were still on the kitchen counter. But you know what? I could not have cared less about a bigger, better, newer house.

In an instant, I came to see what mattered and what didn't.

Suffering makes the things of this world grow strangely dim. We learn not to get worked up over little annoyances when we've walked through great difficulty. It teaches us to hold things loosely and to let go of expectations and entitlement. It teaches the crucial lesson that people matter and things do not.

From that same Roman prison, Paul also wrote about true treasure. "But whatever were gains to me I now consider loss for the sake of Christ. What is more, I consider everything a loss compared to the surpassing greatness of knowing Christ Jesus my Lord, for whose sake I have lost all things. I consider them garbage, that I may gain Christ" (Philippians 3:7–8).

Suffering reminds us of our real home. Imagine an empty jar, and you put one penny into that jar. That penny represents your first day of life. There's still lots of room in the jar. Lots of life yet to live. So now, let's imagine adding a penny for every day you have lived. Depending on how old you are, this jar is getting full.

Now, let's imagine adding more pennies—one penny for each day you'll live until you die. Of course, we don't know how long that will be, but we could take a good guess. If you live to be forty years old, you'll have 14,600 pennies in your jar (not counting leap days for you mathematicians). If you live to be sixty-five, you'll have a jar with 23,725 pennies; if you live to be eighty, you'll have 29,200 pennies; and if you live to be ninety, you'll have 32,850 pennies. You'd need a very large jar.

But we're not done, because life doesn't end when we die. If you're a follower of Christ, your last breath on earth is your first breath in heaven. So add to your jar a penny for each day of your life in heaven. Need another jar? And another? Are you envisioning a roomful of tall jars overflowing with pennies representing eternity?

You'll soon see that trying to imagine the jars of pennies for all the days we'll live in eternity is impossible. As soon as we try to imagine eternity, we've limited it. Our heavenly home with God is forever and ever, without end.

Doing this helps us realize that no matter how many pennies are in our jar at the date of death—from 3,000 to 30,0000—our life on earth is short. Whether it's four or forty or eighty-four years we get on earth, it is a flash compared to all of eternity.

Suffering brings razor-sharp clarity to the fragility of life. It helps strip away so much in this life that is temporary so we can fix our eyes on heaven. Don't get me wrong: Life here is incredible, and God intends us to live it to the hilt. But we can get fixated on living to the hilt without giving weight to what's eternal.

Suffering helps us shift our focus from building our little earthly kingdoms to investing in God's kingdom. It reminds us that suffering is temporary and that "our light and momentary troubles are achieving for us an eternal glory that far outweighs them all" (2 Corinthians 4:17). The Passion Translation puts it like this:

> We view our slight, short-lived troubles in the light of eternity. We see our difficulties as the substance that produces for us an eternal, weighty glory far beyond all comparison, because we don't focus our attention on what is seen but on what is unseen. For what is seen is temporary, but the unseen realm is eternal.
>
> 2 Corinthians 4:17–18 TPT

What God Pours in, We Can Pour Out

As God reshapes our shattered heart, we often realize that it's beating with new purpose. It doesn't come right away. The day-in, day-out work of processing hard emotions, lamenting what's been lost, taming the fear that threatens to paralyze us, and muting the enemy's lies as we find our footing to flourish again is grueling work. When waves of emotion pull us into a pit of despair, it feels like we've taken three steps backward. But walking through that pit is the only way forward. And little by little, those pits become less deep, don't last as long, and are farther and farther apart.

No one can fix our pain for us, but they can comfort us in it. Some of the best comfort, aside from God's presence and his Word, is knowing someone who has walked a similar pain and is a few steps ahead of us. Someone who understands the unique struggles we're facing. Someone who has walked through the worst of it and has hope that life can be good again.

That alone is comfort, but how much more comfort if we don't just see her steps ahead, but if she turns, takes our hand, and helps us walk through the struggle so that we can stand with her on the other side.

Right now, as God comforts you, he is planting seeds of deep compassion. God tells us that "he comforts us in all our troubles so that we can comfort others. When they are troubled, we will be able to give them the same comfort God has given us" (2 Corinthians 1:4 NLT).

God pours his comfort into us so we can turn around and pour comfort out to others.

God pours his comfort into us so we can turn around and pour comfort out to others.

You can be that person who reaches back to help someone a few steps behind you. You'll notice that God begins to bring people into your life who are going through a similar struggle. You will be in a position to uniquely comfort them. There is great comfort in knowing others have experienced difficulty and have emerged with a stronger, deeper faith.

But we won't be stronger just for having suffered. Only when we give God all the pieces of our shattered heart can he reshape us for himself. When we surrender the life we planned, the life we felt entitled to, and trust God, we are ready and open to the life God has for us. While life may dish out unexpected pain, that pain doesn't get the last word. God is sovereign over the unexpected, and when we trust him through it, we will also see unexpected beauty, unexpected gifts, and unexpected good.

I know you wouldn't have chosen this path, friend. The lessons God is teaching you and the character God is shaping in you have come at great cost. But in this hard place, may we let God teach us and refine us in ways we'd never give back.

A Prayer for Good Lessons in Hard Places

Lord, use this hard place for your best work in me. Create in me a clean heart and help me get rid of the sin that has entangled me. Forgive me for holding so tightly to things of this world, my own agenda, and my own expectations. I don't simply want to survive this hard place, Lord. I want to be refined to glorify you, to have a deeper faith, and to be more like Jesus. Give me an eternal perspective as I do the work you've given me here on earth. In Jesus' name, amen.

13

Finding Your Smile in Chapter 2

I would have lost heart, unless I had believed
That I would see the goodness of the LORD
In the land of the living.
Wait on the LORD;
Be of good courage,
And He shall strengthen your heart;
Wait, I say, on the LORD!

Psalm 27:13–14 NKJV

If the day Jesus died was eventually called good, then maybe one day, our worst days might be called good too.

Katherine and Jay Wolf

When you started this book with me, I promised you would smile once again.

So often we think we'll be able to smile again when our circumstances resolve. Once our health is restored, when the marriage is revived, when business turns around, when that relationship heals, or if God will let me remarry, then life will feel good and I'll be able to smile again.

We go to God and pray seriously and persistently for that one thing we think will make our life better and help us feel better. Maybe you're praying for God to send a spouse your way and you just know marriage is the destination that will make life good again. Or maybe you've been praying for a positive pregnancy test or an adoption to come through, and you're certain life will be full and happy when God brings it. Maybe you've been praying for a new work position or a turnaround for your business that would finally make life easy and happy. Or maybe you've prayed for a changed relationship or an open door, and if God would make it happen—because he most certainly could—you would be 100 percent content.

In those first months after Dan died, when I read books by other young widows, I didn't start with chapter 1. I turned to the last chapter because I wanted to know how her story ended. Had she remarried and were her kids thriving? That was the happy ending I thought would get me out of my pain. At the same time, I knew I was setting up a whole new idol in my heart when finding love again was my answer.

If God would only change my circumstances, I could feel good again, we think.

We all want a Cinderella ending to our story. We think the answer to smiling again is moving out of the life that is right now and into the life we want. We want God to wrap our story with the satin bow of happily-ever-after.

But if we pin satisfaction on an outcome, we'll live in continual soul ache.

If we pin satisfaction on an outcome, we'll live in continual soul ache.

If we want to find contentment now, whether or not our circumstances ever change, we have to find satisfaction in God alone.

We have to surrender our happily ever after to God.

This doesn't mean we can't pray and ask God to change our circumstance. God tells us to come to him freely and boldly with our prayer requests, and being in relationship with God means we are safe to bring him our deepest longings.

But so often, our prayer requests become the hinge on which we think a joy-filled life swings open. And while we're waiting for God to bring the outcome we so deeply desire, we hold our breath, skimming through life as it is right now, failing to register that right now matters. We let the life in front of us slip through our fingers because we're waiting for something else to begin.

We need to give our requests to God while surrendering them to his will. Even if God never brings about what we've prayed for, we can find joy right here. Joy is not on hold unless or until something else happens. Your life has full meaning and full purpose right now.

If you are counting on a happily-ever-after outcome to find joy again, I encourage you to pray this prayer of surrender: *Lord, help me want you more than I ever want* ____________.

God will always answer this prayer to put him at the center of our affections. When I realized a certain outcome had become the gateway to the good life for me, I began to pray this prayer over and over until God replaced my obsession for an outcome with himself. You may need to pray it over and over as well. But as you pray, you'll come to realize that your craving for a certain outcome has been replaced by a no-strings-attached request. You'll look around and see that you're content and joyful whether or not God ever brings about that outcome. And you'll be in a place where if God does give you your heart's desire, it will be pure gift. The good life comes when we love God above anything else and when he alone satisfies us.

Of course, knowing that is true doesn't automatically make walking it out easy. It's a process where we learn to hold both of our hands open to God. I imagine myself with both arms extended, both hands open, and palms facing up as if I am doing physically what's taking place spiritually in my heart.

With one hand, we give God the life we'd planned for ourselves. We give him the life we loved that's gone, the life we desperately wanted that never came about, and the dreams we had that haven't been realized. We give him our heart's deepest longings and in full surrender lay them on the altar.

At the same time, we hold our other hand open to what God has for us right now. We ask him to help us embrace the life that is, to find joy here, and to live fully in the life he's given us. We ask him to help us see all the good he has for us here, to find purpose here, and to glorify him in life as he's given it.

To take steps forward through shattering disappointment is to hold both hands open each day. It doesn't mean we don't have good memories of the past or dreams for the future. But holding both hands open to God, we let go of what we don't have while holding ourselves fully open to life as it is now.

Holding both hands open to God, we let go of what we don't have while holding ourselves fully open to life as it is now.

As we hold both hands open, two things can be true at once. I've had friends say they were afraid to move forward because they were leaving behind so much of what they loved. But two things can be true at once.

We can find loveliness in our life even when we don't love what happened.

We can believe God is doing good when we don't feel good.

We can experience joy now even as we're still going through the pain.

We can trust God for what's next even when we don't understand why something happened.

This posture of holding both hands open to God—processing the loss of life as we wanted it and asking God to let us fully live in the life that is—allows us to live in the both/and. The both/and says we don't have to wait to get through something hard to experience something good.

When I posted about this on my Instagram, friends began adding their own both/ands: Erica said you don't have to feel physically well to live a full, beautiful life. Marybeth said you don't have to know the ending to trust God has a plan for you.

If you were to hold both of your hands out to God right now, what would be your both/and? How would you complete this sentence: *I don't have to* ______________ *to* ______________.

This is a choice to not simply live where we are, but to love where we are.

You've done so much hard work as you've processed hard emotions, looked for God's goodness all around you, clung to hope, fought the enemy's lies, and let God chisel out the junk in your heart.

We will miss God's abundance if we're always looking back to what was or craning our neck forward for what might be. Sometimes, we simply need to tell our heart to restart right where we are.

Tell Your Heart to Beat Again

Randy Phillips, the singer and songwriter of the trio Phillips, Craig and Dean, tells the story behind their song "Tell Your Heart to Beat Again." You may have heard it sung by Danny

Gokey of *American Idol* fame, who recorded it later. Phillips says the inspiration for the song came when a pastor attended the open-heart surgery that one of his church members, a cardiac surgeon, was performing. Here's how Phillips described it:

> He's standing in the corner, and they bring the person in. They do this amazing thing where they saw open the chest, open the chest cavity, extract the heart, and then the surgeon begins to do the treatment on the heart, fix the heart, puts the heart back into the chest cavity, and gently massages it. This time, the heart did not start on its own. And so he massaged the heart again. Still nothing happened. And it began to dawn on the pastor, *I may be about to see this surgeon lose this patient.* Then they did a little more treatment on the heart, a little more extreme, to get the heart going. And still nothing.
>
> Finally, the surgeon knelt down beside his patient, and he took off his surgeon's mask and said, "Mrs. Johnson. This is your surgeon. The operation went perfectly. Your heart has been repaired. Now tell your heart to beat again."
>
> And when he said that, the heart began to beat.

Phillips saw the application right away. "There's so many people who've experienced so much brokenness to their heart that even though God, the Great Surgeon, has saved us and repaired us, covered us with his grace, sometimes it takes you and me to tell our own heart, 'Beat again. Love again. Hope again.'"[1]

You might feel stuck in a place of pain, that life will always feel as though it is divided into two halves and you're compelled to live out the half you didn't want. Though it may feel so right now, the painful place is not a cul-de-sac. It's one part of a much longer road that God is walking you along. When you feel stuck in a pain loop, tell your heart to beat again. Remind your heart it will find joy once more.

God Has No Plan B

Though life may look different than you ever expected, it is not unexpected for God. We don't have to understand why God has allowed something to trust him with it.

God does not give us second best. He doesn't serve you the leftovers of a life that should have been five stars. Maybe you think God has given you a stone for a gift.[2] But if we would pick it up and see it for what it is, we would see he has actually given us bread. God cannot give stones.[3]

With God, there are no plan Bs; there are chapter 2s. And while it may not be the chapter you ordered, it's a chapter God foresaw, a chapter God has allowed, and a chapter in which God is fully present. And there is as much abundance and good in this chapter as in all the other chapters that came before. Fully surrendering to God means letting God define what that abundance and good look like.

With God, there are no plan Bs; there are chapter 2s.

The deepest prayer of my heart is that because God has this chapter for me, I will come not just to accept God's will for me, but to agree with it. We may never have our questions answered while on earth. We may never understand why this is the way God has written our story. But we can be sure that God is always right. That God is for us and that he is only kind and always good.

Let's not miss all that God has for us here because we've got our hands clenched around the life we wanted. Keep fighting for joy. Keep looking for God's goodness all around you. Trust that God is reshaping the shattered pieces of your life into something far beyond what you could ask or imagine. You will find your smile again.

A Prayer for Your Chapter 2

Dear God, I come to you wanting to surrender anything in my life I've placed above you. Help me find deep satisfaction in you alone, whether or not you ever bring about what I've prayed for. I give it to you and trust that your ways are best and they are right. Help me hold both hands open to you, to let go of the life I wanted and to take hold of all that you have for me here. Restore my joy in this chapter and do not let me miss what you're doing here and now. I love you with all my heart, all my soul, all my mind, all my strength. Help me to love you more. In Jesus' name, amen.

Appendix A

40 Promises of God

God is attentive.

Psalm 10:17—You, LORD, hear the desire of the afflicted; you encourage them, and you listen to their cry.

1 John 5:14–15—This is the confidence we have in approaching God: that if we ask anything according to his will, he hears us. And if we know that he hears us—whatever we ask—we know that we have what we asked of him.

God is compassionate.

Psalm 116:5–6—The LORD is gracious and righteous; our God is full of compassion. The LORD protects the unwary; when I was brought low, he saved me.

1 Peter 5:7—Cast all your anxiety on him because he cares for you.

God comforts us.

John 14:16—And I will ask the Father, and he will give you another advocate to help you and be with you forever.

2 Corinthians 1:3–4—Praise be to the God and Father of our Lord Jesus Christ, the Father of compassion and the God of all comfort, who comforts us in all our troubles, so that we can comfort those in any trouble with the comfort we ourselves receive from God.

God is faithful.

Psalm 9:10—Those who know your name trust in you, for you, LORD, have never forsaken those who seek you.

Isaiah 25:1—LORD, you are my God; I will exalt you and praise your name, for in perfect faithfulness you have done wonderful things, things planned long ago.

1 Thessalonians 5:24—The one who calls you is faithful, and he will do it.

God brings good fruit from difficulty.

John 15:5—I am the vine; you are the branches. If you remain in me and I in you, you will bear much fruit; apart from me you can do nothing.

James 1:2–3—Consider it pure joy, my brothers and sisters, whenever you face trials of many kinds, because you know that the testing of your faith produces perseverance.

Hebrews 12:10–11—God disciplines us for our good, in order that we may share in his holiness. No discipline seems pleasant at the time, but painful. Later on, however, it produces a harvest of righteousness and peace for those who have been trained by it.

Galatians 6:9—Let us not become weary in doing good, for at the proper time we will reap a harvest if we do not give up.

God is good and does good.

Psalm 27:13—I remain confident of this: I will see the goodness of the LORD in the land of the living.

Psalm 86:5—You, Lord, are forgiving and good, abounding in love to all who call to you.

Psalm 119:68—You are good, and what you do is good.

God guides us.

Psalm 32:8—I will instruct you and teach you in the way you should go; I will counsel you with my loving eye on you.

Proverbs 3:5–6—Trust in the LORD with all your heart and lean not on your own understanding; in all your ways submit to him, and he will make your paths straight.

Isaiah 48:17—This is what the LORD says—your Redeemer, the Holy One of Israel: "I am the LORD your God, who teaches you what is best for you, who directs you in the way you should go."

God gives us hope.

1 Peter 1:3–4—Praise be to the God and Father of our Lord Jesus Christ! In his great mercy he has given us

new birth into a living hope through the resurrection of Jesus Christ from the dead, and into an inheritance that can never perish, spoil or fade. This inheritance is kept in heaven for you.

Jeremiah 29:11—"For I know the plans I have for you," declares the Lord, "plans to prosper you and not to harm you, plans to give you hope and a future."

God always loves.

1 Corinthians 13:8—Love never fails.

Psalm 136:26—Give thanks to the God of heaven. *His love endures forever.*

God gives us peace.

Isaiah 26:3—You will keep in perfect peace those whose minds are steadfast, because they trust in you.

Philippians 4:7—And the peace of God, which transcends all understanding, will guard your hearts and your minds in Christ Jesus.

Psalm 4:8—In peace I will lie down and sleep, for you alone, Lord, make me dwell in safety.

God is present with us.

Psalm 34:18—The Lord is close to the brokenhearted and saves those who are crushed in spirit.

James 4:8—Come near to God and he will come near to you.

Hebrews 13:5—God has said, "Never will I leave you; never will I forsake you."

God provides for all our needs.

Philippians 4:19—And my God will meet all your needs according to the riches of his glory in Christ Jesus.

2 Corinthians 9:8—And God is able to bless you abundantly, so that in all things at all times, having all that you need, you will abound in every good work.

God is a refuge in troubled times.

Psalm 9:9—The LORD is a refuge for the oppressed, a stronghold in times of trouble.

Deuteronomy 33:27—The eternal God is your refuge, and underneath are the everlasting arms.

God restores joy for us.

Psalm 30:5—For his anger lasts only a moment, but his favor lasts a lifetime; weeping may stay for the night, but rejoicing comes in the morning.

Psalm 126:5–6—Those who sow with tears will reap with songs of joy. Those who go out weeping, carrying seed to sow, will return with songs of joy, carrying sheaves with them.

Psalm 94:19—When anxiety was great within me, your consolation brought me joy.

God is a shield to us.

Psalm 84:11—For the LORD God is a sun and shield; the LORD bestows favor and honor; no good thing does he withhold from those whose walk is blameless.

Genesis 15:1—"Do not be afraid, Abram. I am your shield, your very great reward."

God sustains us.

Psalm 94:18—When I said, "My foot is slipping," your unfailing love, LORD, supported me.

Psalm 27:5—For in the day of trouble he will keep me safe in his dwelling; he will hide me in the shelter of his sacred tent and set me high upon a rock.

Psalm 3:5—I lie down and sleep; I wake again, because the LORD sustains me.

Jeremiah 17:7–8—But blessed is the one who trusts in the LORD, whose confidence is in him. They will be like a tree planted by the water that sends out its roots by the stream. It does not fear when heat comes; its leaves are always green. It has no worries in a year of drought and never fails to bear fruit.

You can download all forty promises of God at LisaAppelo.com/BookExtras

Appendix B

Grace Guide for Hard Seasons

1. Wake to new morning mercies.
2. Let grace govern your self-talk.
3. Lean on moment-by-moment grace.
4. Allow grace to reign in your relationships.
5. Count on God's strength to show up in weakness.
6. Trust the future to God and do the next thing now.
7. Let yourself off the hook of high expectations.
8. Remember it won't always feel like this.
9. Rebuild beauty one step at a time.
10. Persist in prayer.

If you'd like to download a copy of the extended Grace Guide for Hard Seasons—a list of declarations to let grace guide you and your family when life falls apart—you can find it at LisaAppelo.com/BookExtras.

Notes

Chapter 1 This Is Too Hard. I Cannot Do This.

1. C. H. Spurgeon, "Israel's God and God's Israel," Metropolitan Tabernacle, Sermon 803, Spurgeon Gems, http://www.spurgeongems.org/sermon/chs803.pdf.

Chapter 2 Your Emotions Are Welcome Here

1. Mark 3:5.
2. Isaiah 53:3.
3. Matthew 4:11.
4. Mark 15:34.
5. John 4:6.
6. HELPS Word-studies, cognate 1145, Bible Hub, 2021, https://biblehub.com/greek/1145.htm.
7. HELPS Word-studies, cognate 2906, Bible Hub, 2021, https://biblehub.com/greek/2906.htm.
8. Mandy Oaklander, "The Science of Crying," *Time*, March 16, 2016, https://time.com/4254089/science-crying/.
9. Judith Orloff, MD, "The Health Benefits of Tears," *Psychology Today*, July 27, 2010, https://www.psychologytoday.com/us/blog/emotional-freedom/201007/the-health-benefits-tears.
10. Ashley Marcin, "9 Ways Crying May Benefit Your Health," Healthline, April 14, 2017, https://www.healthline.com/health/benefits-of-crying.
11. Orloff, "The Health Benefits of Tears."

Chapter 3 The Great Exchange

1. "In the past God spoke to our ancestors through the prophets at many times and in various ways, but in these last days he has spoken to us by his Son, whom he appointed heir of all things, and through whom also he made the universe" (Hebrews 1:1–2).

2. I followed the Robert Murray M'Cheyne Bible reading plan, which takes the reader through four passages each day, covering the Old Testament once and the Psalms and New Testament twice during the year. See http://www.edginet.org/mcheyne/info.html.

3. Strong's Exhaustive Concordance, 4478, Bible Hub, https://biblehub.com/hebrew/4478.htm.

4. Esther Fleece, *No More Faking Fine: Ending the Pretending* (Grand Rapids: Zondervan, 2017), 106.

5. Esther Fleece, *No More Faking Fine*, 106.

6. Romans 8:26 ESV.

7. Mark Vroegop, *Dark Clouds, Deep Mercy: Discover the Grace of Lament* (Wheaton: Crossway, 2019), 28.

Chapter 4 Find Your Footing

1. I'm indebted to Dr. Donald McCall "Mac" Brunson for teaching the nature of God's faithfulness.

2. Billy Graham, *The Journey* (Nashville: W Publishing, 2006), 68.

3. Victor Knowles, "Promise and Fulfillment: Believing the Promises of God," *Poverty and Possessions* 6, no. 3 (1998): Article 4, https://digitalcommons.pepperdine.edu/cgi/viewcontent.cgi?article=1769&context=leaven.

4. Joshua 1:3.

5. Philippians 4:19.

Chapter 5 The God Who Is for You

1. 1 Corinthians 2:14.

2. "The Attributes of God—Study Resources," Blue Letter Bible, www.blueletterbible.org/faq/attributes.cfm

3. Psalm 34:18.

4. This has been a bedrock principle since I first encountered it in the Bible study by Henry Blackaby, Richard Blackaby, and Claude King, *Experiencing God: Knowing and Doing the Will of God* (Nashville: Lifeway Press, 1990).

5. Job 26:14.

6. Isaiah 49:16.

Chapter 7 Desperate for Good in a Life Gone Bad

1. Genesis 2:17.

2. Genesis 3:1.

3. Genesis 3:3.

4. Genesis 3:4–5.

5. Winston Smith, "Learning to Be Thankful Even When I'm Told I Have to Be," CCEF, November 20, 2015, https://www.ccef.org/learning-be-thankful-even-when-im-told-i-have-be/.

6. Revelation 4:8–10.

Chapter 8 Crush Your Fear

1. Alli Worthington, *Fierce Faith: A Woman's Guide to Fighting Fear, Wrestling Worry, and Overcoming Anxiety* (Grand Rapids: Zondervan, 2017), 19.

Chapter 9 The Enemy in the Midst of This

1. HELPS Word-studies, cognate 1228, Bible Hub, 2021, https://biblehub.com/greek/1228.htm.

2. HELPS Word-studies, cognate 476, Bible Hub, 2021, https://biblehub.com/greek/476.htm.

3. Thayer's Greek Lexicon, Strong's NT 3985, Bible Hub, 2021, https://biblehub.com/greek/3985.htm.

4. Revelation 12:10.

5. HELPS Word-studies, cognate 3180, Bible Hub, 2021, https://biblehub.com/greek/3180.htm.

6. HELPS Word-studies, cognate 2540, Bible Hub, 2021, https://biblehub.com/greek/2540.htm.

7. David Platt, *Exalting Jesus in Matthew: Christ-Centered Exposition Commentary* (B&H Publishing, 2013), ch. 8.

8. Priscilla Shirer, *The Armor of God* (Nashville: Lifeway Press, 2020), 43.

9. Shirer, *The Armor of God*, 95.

10. Strong's Concordance, 2091, Bible Hub, 2021, https://biblehub.com/greek/2091.htm.

11. HELPS Word-studies, cognate 5287, Bible Hub, 2021, https://biblehub.com/greek/5287.htm.

12. Neringa Antanaityte, "Mind Matters: How to Effortlessly Have More Positive Thoughts," TLEX Institute, https://tlexinstitute.com/how-to-effortlessly-have-more-positive-thoughts/.

13. Tony Evans, *Victory in Spiritual Warfare* (Eugene, OR: Harvest House Publishers, 2011), 137.

Chapter 10 Hanging On to Threadbare Hope

1. Pam Tebow, *Hope for a Woman's Heart: 52 Encouraging Devotions* (Tyndale Momentum, 2021), 6.

2. Romans 15:13.

3. G. K. Chesterton, *Heretics* (New York: John Lane Company, 1905), 119.

4. Genesis 12:1–2.

5. Genesis 17:16, 21.

6. Lindsey Wheeler with Mary Carver, *Sacred Tears: Simple Reminders that God Sees You and Loves You* (Eugene: Harvest House Publishers, 2021), 55.

Chapter 12 Let God Reshape Your Shattered Heart

1. Elisabeth Elliot, *Suffering Is Never for Nothing* (Nashville: B&H Publishing Group, 2019).

2. Kay Arthur, *As Silver Refined: Learning to Embrace Life's Disappointments* (Colorado Springs: Waterbrook Press, 1997), 3.

Chapter 13 Finding Your Smile in Chapter 2

1. Fair Trade Services, "Phillips, Craig & Dean Introduces Their New Song," 2:33, May 9, 2012, https://www.youtube.com/watch?v=pdPp7ofeBMA.

2. Matthew 7:9.

3. Elisabeth Elliot, "Bread, Not Stones," Blue Letter Bible, www.blueletterbible.org/audio_video/popPlayer.cfm?id=16090&rel=elliot_elisabeth/misc.

Acknowledgments

Lord, thank you for rescuing me. In my deepest pain, you didn't just make it bearable. You entered it with me and let me see so much of your glory that I never wanted to leave your sweet presence. You have been true to every word and faithful to every promise. I thought I loved you then; help me love you more.

To Ben and Elizabeth, Rachel and David, Nicholas and Colette, Seth and Grace, Zachary and Erica, Matthew, and Annalise, you have brought life and laughter and joy. To my seven, you have walked the hardest hard, extended grace when I fought to get my footing again, and loved each other well. Thank you for believing and cheering this call to write when it felt like crazy faith. I love you so incredibly. Matt and Annalise, I promise to start cooking again.

To Mom and Dad, you are the absolute best. I can't even begin to thank you for everything you've done. Thank you for the sacrificial love and support you've always shown, but especially in these last ten years. Thank you for field trip days so I could write. You never had to move next door, but I'm glad we're down the road now. And to Sherri and Ira, Jeff and Cacky, thank you for being there and for all the ways you have loved the kids and me so well.

To Abby, Kristi, Kristine, Lyli, Betsy, and Tiffany, thank you for being a safe place to dream and grow in writing. Thank you for authentic conversations, shared insight, deep encouragement, and so many prayers.

To Lynn, Glenn, Teresa, Howdy, Karen, Ron, Michelle, John, Pam, Mark, Rhonda, John, Vicki, Brad, Stephanie, Theresa, David, our Elijah Family, our Grove Bluff neighbors, and so many friends who showed up on our worst day: You were the hands and feet of Jesus for us that day and so many days after. You taught me what it means to just go, be present, look for ways to help, and show up.

To William and Barbara, Skip and Peggy, Martin and Ann, true to your character, you have gone above and beyond to support, encourage, love, and help our family in the wake of Dan's death in countless ways. It has meant the world. To Dan's Coastal Construction Products family, he thought the world of you. Thank you for making work days incredible days, and for making work relationships feel more like family.

To so many from our beloved FBC Jacksonville family, the middle school department, and my ladies Sunday school class. You formed and shaped us and will forever be a part of our family. Thank you for loving us in ways I probably still don't even know, for your faithfulness, your prayers, and your practical help long after most would have forgotten. You wept with us as we wept, and modeled how to love the hurting. Thank you to Dan and Marianne Elkins for pastoring my children so well, to Dr. Brunson for pastoring our family so faithfully, and teachers who left an eternal mark on our family: Jeff, Dave, Tad, Brian, Sandy, among so many others. To my Sunday school crew: Our time in God's Word and in life together was pure gift and serving alongside you was my week's highlight. I'm forever grateful for your friendship. Adrienne and Bill, who knew faithful servants could be such refreshing fun?

To Sarah Lango, Teresa Russell, Rhonda Ellis, Eleana Simmons, Jennifer Uren, and Jodi Rosser, thank you for letting me share your stories and for inspiring me personally with your faith through life's storms.

To Niki, Kate, Dena, Ronne, and Michele, thank you for your wise counsel, sharp insight, and God-honoring hearts.

To Brittany Price Booker, Vaneetha Rendall Risner, Becky Keife, Suzanne Eller, Kia Stephens, Michelle Nietert, Niki Hardy, Dorina Gilmore Young, and Dr. Michelle Bengtson, thank you for reading an early copy of this manuscript and your investment of time to help cheer on this book.

To Blythe McIntosh Daniel, your input and vision for this book helped shape it in the earliest days. Thank you for cheering it and me on, for your prayers and your friendship.

To the team at Bethany House Publishers: Jennifer Dukes Lee—what a privilege to work with someone I've admired for so long. Thank you for believing in this message. And to the rest of the incredible Bethany House, thank you for shaping this book through your art and skill. What an honor to get to publish words with you to impact the world for Christ.

About the Author

Lisa Appelo is a speaker, writer, and Bible teacher who inspires women to cultivate faith in life's storms. She's a Florida girl born and raised, and she followed her passion for writing into law, where she worked as a litigator for many years. As her family grew to include seven children, Lisa retired from law to raise and home educate her children.

Ten years ago, Lisa went to bed happily married to her high school sweetheart and woke up a widow and single mom. As she navigated grief and shepherded her children through their own grief, God reshaped all that seemed shattered. Lisa is passionate about rich Bible study and taught a weekly ladies' Bible class at her home church for many years. She launched a local ministry for widows in Jacksonville, Florida, and co-founded the Facebook group Widow Mama Collective. Lisa writes at LisaAppelo.com and manages a team of writers at HopeinGrief.com. She's been published at Proverbs 31 Ministries, (in)courage, Risen Motherhood, and Jennifer Rothschild, and has been a contributing writer for iMOM.com, The Life of a Single Mom, and Sweet to the Soul Faith Journal.

Her days are filled top to bottom with stewarding her precious children, writing, ministry, speaking, and walking enough to justify lots of dark chocolate. Connect with Lisa at LisaAppelo.com and on Instagram @lisaappelo.